Sent from the Father

Sent from the Father

Meditations on the Fourth Gospel

José Comblin

Translated by Carl Kabat

ORBIS BOOKS
Maryknoll, New York 10545

Second Printing, June 1981

Library of Congress Cataloging in Publication Data

Comblin, Joseph, 1923–
    Sent from the Father.

    Translation of O Enviado do Pai.
    1. Bible. N.T. John—Meditations. I. Title.
BS2615.4.C6413   226'.5'06   78-16750
ISBN 0-88344-453-4

The Catholic Foreign Mission Society of America (Maryknoll) recruits and trains people for overseas missionary service. Through Orbis Books Maryknoll aims to foster the international dialogue that is essential to mission. The books published, however, reflect the opinions of their authors and are not meant to represent the official position of the Society.

First published as *O enviado do pai*, copyright © 1974 by Editora Vozes Ltda., Rua Frei Luís, 100, 25.600, Petrópolis, RJ, Brazil

English translation copyright © 1979 by Orbis Books, Maryknoll, NY 10545

Scriptural quotations are taken from *The New English Bible.* © The Delegates of the Oxford University Press and the Syndics of the Cambridge University Press 1961, 1970. Reprinted by permission.

Printed in the United States of America

CONTENTS

Preface

The originality of the Gospel according to John consists in this: The author extracts from the tradition about Jesus certain themes and presents these in all their aspects and all their relationships. In a sense the entire substance of the Fourth Gospel consists of fifteen words, and Jesus' discourses in the Fourth Gospel concern all the possible connections among these fifteen words. These fifteen words are the following:

father (119 times)   glory (38 times)
sent (41 times)   to know (88 times)
man (35 times)   disciples (77 times)
world (77 times)   to believe (43 times)
to do (36 times)   truth (55 times)
works (21 times)   love (44 times)
signs (16 times)   life (52 times)
testimony (46 times)

It is as if the last apostle of the apostolic generation desires to fix indelibly in the memory of following generations the light that emanated from Jesus. To this end he reiterates and rephrases ceaselessly a Christian message of the most radical originality clothed in the simplest and most ordinary diction. This presentation simultaneously exalts Jesus and renders him universally accessible.

All the themes of the Fourth Gospel are presented in the person of Jesus. The Christian message is not presented as a philosophy, a code of law or ethics, a doctrine, a catechism: it appears in the person of Jesus and in the impact of his presence on others. It was the author's purpose to transmit that presence and that impact to following generations.

In accord with his purpose John portrays a Jesus of incomparable unity and simplicity of character. At every moment, in every act, in every circumstance, he was always himself: the one "sent from the Father," the "missionary" who is never more nor less than a missionary, he who unites the Father and the world not as a bridge joins two fixed points, but by means of a movement, a passage, a communication between living beings.

Thus the title of this work: Sent from the Father. The theme of mission is primary; it is the organizing principle of the message of the Fourth Gospel. Thus we begin our meditations on this theme. We examine subsequent themes in the light of mission, for it is mission that gives them a particular orientation in John's Gospel.

1

"That the world may believe that thou didst send me"

THE ONE SENT

Who is Jesus? The Fourth Gospel is essentially an answer to this question. But Jesus himself, in the Fourth Gospel, did not give his name or characterize himself. He did not say who he was; he told only whence he came and where he was going.

Jesus is he who came from the Father and was sent by him: "I come from him and he it is who sent me" (7:29); he was sent by the Father, and he came to the world: "He entered his own realm" (1:11).

"The one sent" is the name by which Jesus can be identified: "This is eternal life: to know thee who alone art truly God, and Jesus Christ

1

whom thou hast sent" (17:3). "Thou hast sent me into the world" (17:18), said Jesus to the Father in recapitulation of his entire existence. The disciples began to know him at the moment they understood that he was sent: "And these men know that thou didst send me" (17:25). The world can know Jesus only in the same way, by grasping his "being sent": "That the world may believe that thou didst send me" (17:21).

In referring to God, Jesus almost always said, "the Father who sent me" (5:23,37), or simply "him who sent me" (5:24,30; 6:38). Just as Jesus designated God as the sender, he designated himself as the one sent. Instead of "I," he spoke of "he that the Father sent": "This is the work that God requires: believe in the one whom he has sent" (6:29).

This mission—this "being sent" by God —distinguishes Jesus' role from all others in the world. If a professor, for example, is "sent," or appointed, to teach physics, it is the physics that is essential. The particular professor and teaching methods are incidental, so long as the understanding of physics is conveyed. Put even more simply, mail carriers, whatever their personal qualities, are incidental to the messages in the letters they bring. As mail carriers, they are merely the medium by which the messages arrive. But in the case of Jesus, the reverse is true: Jesus, who was sent by the

Father, does not bring a message; he is the message. He does not convey truth; he is truth. The Father did not send Jesus to bring a gift to humanity; he sent Jesus to humanity.

Furthermore, our hypothetical physics professor and mail carriers possess personal attributes, apart from their respective functions, that may interest us. But Jesus, in the Fourth Gospel, is solely and entirely he who was sent. His whole being is a communication between God and the world.

The nature of Jesus as he who was sent is the key to the interpretation of the Fourth Gospel and of the Christian message. Jesus as sent by God reveals to us a new way of being human, or rather, a way of being authentically human. John thus exposes the self-satisfaction and superficiality of humanistic definitions of being human.

By defining Jesus as one who was sent, John is not emphasizing that he entered the world at a particular point in time to begin to function as savior. Quite the contrary. Jesus *is* the one sent. He was, is, and will be sent to humankind. His very being is missionary. By defining Jesus in terms of his mission, John correctly shows that the way to be authentically human is to be as one sent by God.

We humans, at least we westerners, tend to perceive and define ourselves by what demarcates and separates us from others. Our consciousness of "person" much resembles our consciousness of "ownership." Thence it is a relatively short step to the definition of self in terms of possessions. Capitalist society in particular exacerbates this tendency to perceive oneself in terms of one's possessions and therefore to *accumulate* in order to *be*. Thinking that one *is* only by virtue of what one *has* necessarily engenders egocentrism—a desire for sole possession of one's defining attributes. Others are a threat to one's possessions and one's person and must therefore be rejected, "fenced out." The insecurity resulting from the confusion of personhood with ownership prevents us from seeing that the desire for autonomy leads in fact to the extinction of personhood.

Jesus was just the opposite. He was nothing in himself or for himself. He had no possessions; therefore, he needed no walls against others. He was wholly the channel by which God communicates himself to the world. Autonomy was Jesus' antithesis. Through him passed the contact between God and humanity, and he subsisted in this movement. He was open to the Father and open to the world, not closed up within himself. He existed as relation, and had no other being or personality than to be communication between the Father and humanity. That was Jesus' mission, and in the exercise of his mission lay his authentic humanity. His was the "missionary" way of being human.

No part of the evangelical narration shows Jesus self-absorbed; he simply does not appear outside his relationships with God and with other people. He can be called *logos*, that is, "word," or "voice," because he was always word, either reception or emission of word; he was the resonance of the word of the Father. Except as word, Jesus had no existence.

Clearly Jesus is the antithesis of humanist egocentrism. For us love is a virtue, or an obligation, or an aspiration, or a challenge, or a satisfaction; for us love is merely an accompaniment of "I." It is never the whole content or definition of "I." In Jesus love and self were one; he had no private self in isolation, separate from his love.

But Jesus was never meant to be the only missionary; John says that God explicitly did not intend Jesus to be unique. On the contrary, Jesus' mode of existence as mission made manifest furnished the model for all the disciples. We must understand in their fullest and most radical sense Jesus' words: "As thou hast sent me into the world, I have sent them into the world" (17:18); and after the Resurrection: "As the Father sent me, so I send you" (20:21), that is to say, "As the Father made me a missionary, so I make you missionaries."

In the Fourth Gospel there are no differences between the description of Jesus, the description of the church, and the description of the disciples. Christology includes them all: If we understand Jesus, we understand the disciples and the church as well.

HE HEARD

Missionaries are in the first place persons oriented toward the Father, those who remain wholly and continually attentive and entirely receptive to him, those who hear him. They have nothing of their own, only what they have received. Therefore their perceptions differ totally from ordinary, habitual human perceptions. We normally consider personality to be something that is "ours," therefore something to be protected against others. We confuse personality with immanence. Science and philosophy are considered as an expression of what is already within us. It is simple enough to do: We make the criterion of any new idea or message its conformability with what is already considered true. Then the search for truth becomes only the reformulation of what we already think is true, and wisdom consists in knowing that there can be nothing new.

But Jesus proposed inverting this attitude. He proposed going beyond the self in the search for truth, being hopeful of and receptive to a transcendent truth. Jesus did not speak of who he was; he spoke of what he had received.

The Fourth Gospel utterly negates immanence: No one discovers God by reflection on self; neither can one know God by contemplating people. The person who contemplates self discovers only self and vanity and learns nothing about either God or people.

All Jesus' negations are radical: "I do not mean that anyone has seen the Father. He who has come from God has seen the Father, and he alone" (6:46). The Jews themselves, who meditated every day on the words of the sacred books, did not know the Father. They made the words into a property, their own goods; they contemplated the words, and in the words thus appropriated and transformed into their own property they heard only their own voices. They believed that they heard God, but only heard themselves. To hear God it is necessary to leave off listening to yourself and to abide in a pure hope, in a pure listening, to be disposed to receive something new. Jesus' rebuke to the Jews could not have outraged them more: "You never heard his voice, or saw his form. . . . His word has found no home in you" (5:37).

It is not enough to search the Scriptures. The church itself was transformed into Christendom; it treated the word of God as its property and tried to encase the kingdom of God in its own institutions. Christians, believing that they had in themselves the face of God, consequently thought that to be faithful to themselves was to be faithful to God. The church concluded that its service to God was to perpetuate and magnify itself. It did not know God. It ceased knowing him at the moment it ceased listening and learning and began, instead, repeating to itself the words of God that it had already heard.

Jesus is he who continually hears and sees, he who lives by receiving. All that he has is received: "I have taught them all that I learned from thee" (17:8). He says to his disciples:

I have disclosed to you everything that I heard from my Father (15:15).

I do not speak on my own authority, but the Father who sent me has himself commanded me what to say and how to speak. . . . What the Father has said to me, therefore—that is what I speak (12:49–50).

The Son can do nothing by himself; he does only what he sees the Father doing: what the Father does, the Son does (5:19).

I cannot act by myself; I judge as I am bidden (5:30).

He whom God sent utters the words of God, so measureless is God's gift of the Spirit (3:34).

Egocentrism leads people to believe (even if they have not the temerity to say so) that they have originated all that they do and are. Jesus, in contrast, knew that nothing of what he did or said or was came from himself; he referred his whole existence to the Father. The missionary does not transmit anything of self, only what has been received from God.

WE KNOW

Most of us seek security by creating an autonomous, closed, personal universe—in other words, an egocentric universe—in which we hope to conceal our profound insecurity and the futility of our knowledge. Since our safety seems to lie within this universe, we defend it strenuously against external messages or questioning. But Jesus knew that his message was from without and was capable of changing the human condition. He knew that his word was endowed with a radical authority and was indestructible precisely because it did not proceed from himself but from the Father. His mission was the transmission of the force and the authority of the Father to the world. The Father's message passed through him to the world like the sun through a clear window. Since, therefore, Jesus did not need the false security of a closed, autonomous universe, he was sovereignly free, open, and secure. His purpose for the disciples was to refashion them in his own image, not as depositories of a magic power or formula, but as people who knew that through them, through their action, passed the Father's message, that the Father acted and affirmed his authority through them.

Jesus was the Son who received everything from the Father:

> The Father loves the Son and shows him all his work (5:20).
> My testimony is valid, even though I do bear witness about myself; because I know where I come from and where I am going (8:14).
> We speak of what we know, and testify to what we have seen (3:11).
> He who comes from heaven bears witness to what he has seen and heard, yet no one accepts his witness (3:32).
> I know him because I come from him and he it is who sent me (7:29).
> You do not know him. But I know him (8:55).
> I am revealing in words what I saw in my Father's presence (8:38).
> O Righteous Father, although the world does not know thee, I know thee, and these men know that thou didst send me (17:25).

Jesus was in himself a gift received from the Father and a manifestation of that gift. To this relation, Jesus gave the name of love. "The Father loves the Son and has entrusted him with all authority" (3:35). The Father's love in no way partook of wanting or possessing. It was the love of giving. In himself the Son was nothing and had nothing that the Father could want. He was the gift received, and the love consisted in an unequal relationship and in two correlative attitudes: that which was open to give and that which was open to receive.

In Jesus was manifested the Father's love and the Father in his love. Therefore Jesus was able to say to Philip: "Anyone who has seen me has seen the Father. Then how can you say: 'Show us the Father?' Do you not believe that I am in the Father, and the Father in me? I am not myself the source of the words I speak to you: it is the Father who dwells in me doing his own work" (14:9–10).

We must understand, however, that Jesus did not know the Father as the Father knows himself. Nor, therefore, could the disciples—or we ourselves—participate in the Father's self-knowledge. Still less can we know the Father "objectively" or "scientifically," as outside observers of a discrete reality. There exists no objective knowledge of the Father. Jesus knew the Father and his love in his experience as Son, as one who received, heard, and saw; he knew this love by being loved and by receiving knowledge. Jesus knew the Father as a son knows, as the origin and content of his mission, as the authority and fount of reality of all that he transmitted. His knowledge of the Father was intrinsic to his mission and experienced in his mission.

The disciples likewise knew the Father and his love in the act of living the missionary condition. They knew him in that receptivity, in that continual attention, in that emptying of self that is necessary to receive knowledge of the Father. In their mission, their condition of "being sent," Jesus' prayer for them was realized: "I made thy name known to them, and will make it known, so that the love thou hadst for me may be in them, and I may be in them" (17:9); "then the world will learn that thou didst send me, that thou didst love them as thou didst me" (17:23).

The Father's love for the disciples was transmitted and manifested in and through the love of Jesus. Jesus' love communicated the Father's love. Likewise, the disciples love will manifest both the love of Jesus and the love of the Father. A current of love arises in which each receives in order to give: "As the Father has loved me, so I have loved you" (15:9); "love one another, as I have loved you" (15:12).

The church participates in the mission of the Son: Its function is to have life only by and through the authority of the Father, to be constantly receptive to the Father, to be the transparent vehicle of revelation of the Father's love.

As such the church is neither institution nor community, though it possesses characteristics of both. The church's validity lies in its mission: in transmitting the Father's love and will to the world. If the church makes of itself an institution, it succeeds as the Pharisees succeeded: It turns God's words into its own property, into a code of laws, customs, and formulas with which to identify; believing that it is contemplating God, it contemplates itself. The church is even less a community in the ordinary sense: Its authentic existence does not derive from the coming together of certain people but from common submission and obedience to the Father's word and work. Recognition of the Father's authority defines the only sense in which the church is a community. Because of this the church as community could never be regulated as human communities are regulated.

People become truly human in the measure that they are open to the Word and also to the world. We must now determine what comprises openness to the world.

HE CAME INTO THE WORLD

Coming to the world is the third phase of mission, completing the movement that begins with being sent and continues through always hearing God's word. Jesus was sent, and he fulfilled his mission: He came. Just as it emphasizes his "being sent" and his receptiveness, the Fourth Gospel stresses Jesus' coming: "I came from the Father and have come into the world" (16:28); "from him I come. I have not come of my own accord; he sent me" (8:42). Martha confessed: "I now believe that you are the Messiah, the Son of God who was to come into the world" (11:27). "I came" and "I came to the world," express the third aspect of mission. Like being sent and being receptive, entering the world defines Jesus' way of being: He came to us permanently.

He came where? To a world not totally new to him, for he already "was in the world" (1:10). "Through him all things came to be; no single thing was created without him" (1:3); "he entered his own realm" (1:11).

But "his own would not receive him (1:11), and "the world . . . did not recognize him" (1:10). He was not expected, or recognized, or received with honor. The people among whom he came did not, for the most part, recognize the exact consonance between Jesus' words and their own deepest selves.

Nevertheless, uninvited, Jesus came. A missionary cannot, by definition, wait for an invitation or the likelihood of a favorable reception. The mission cannot await its moment, for such a moment would never come; it must create its own moment by its own act.

The contemporary human sciences stress the differences between cultures and the difficulties of communication between them. Certainly linguistic history points to the creation of separate, relatively self-contained, and mutually antagonistic cultures. According to this theory Christianity, originating outside human culture entirely, might be shown by science to be entirely incomprehensible to and incompatible with this world.

This doctrine of cultural impermeability has sometimes led the church to assume that evangelization has no chance of success unless like speaks to like. The Gospel tends to show, on the contrary, that radical evangelization can only be the work of a stranger. A message from like to like usually becomes a form of monologue: The listeners hear with pleasure and satisfaction, because they hear their own words and recognize themselves. In these conditions no evangelization is possible. Someone must come from outside with news that makes unprecedented demands on the listener. Jesus was such a stranger, and so must all missionaries be strangers. They must not attempt to hide their alien condition. Jesus did not send his disciples to their own kind only but to all the nations of the world, to peoples completely alien to them.

Mission, however, is not a meeting of two cultures or the translation of one culture into another. Mission is a movement that begins at a point beyond any culture—the Father's love—and arrives at a point beyond any culture with people beyond all their defensive systems, completely disarmed and open and receptive to one another. Constituents of culture can assist the evangelization process, but they often can be more a hindrance than a help. To believe in mission is to believe in the possibility of being authentically human and to do works that are particular to no one culture, but are authentically and universally human. Jesus' acts and way of being are not expressions of a particular culture, but transmit a reality comprehensible by all people. To believe in mission is also to believe that all people possess a fundamental openness, a capacity to receive messages from outside their culture and all cultures. To believe in mission is to believe that humanity is prisoned within itself.

Jesus lived in relation to the Father, from whom he received the totality of his being, and in relation to the world, to which he transmitted the totality of his being. Thus he rendered twofold obedience and fidelity in one mode of being: to serving wholly as passage, transmission, movement from the Father to the world. Missionaries see and hear that they may dispose and enable others to see and hear. The love spoken of in the Fourth Gospel is in no way circular; it is an ongoing current and communication. To love is to transmit what one has received; to give, not what was originally one's own, but what one has been given by another; to receive, and to communicate what is received, so that the movement from the Father to the world continues.

Jesus said, "My Father and I are one" (10:30); "the Father is in me and I in the Father" (10:38). Jesus prayed: "May they all be one: as thou, Father, art in me, and I in thee, so also may they be in us" (17:21). This unity is not a reduction to identity; the unity that exists between Father and Son proceeds from the movement of communication between Father and Son, between the one who sent and the one who was sent; their two modes of being are complementary and form a dynamic unity. In the same manner the unity that Jesus prayed for, among all people and between

Father and Son and all people, is not identity or sameness but results from the movement and circulation of divine love.

In an institution, unity results from the submission of all to the same structure, from imposing on all the same attitudes transformed into custom; authority is derived from the institution, and the leaders are servants of the institution. In a community, unity results from the agreement or the converging interests of all the members, and authority is derived from the common will; the leaders act in the name of the community members. In the church of Jesus Christ unity is derived from the movement that proceeds from the Father to the world. Every member is a link in that current. Everyone receives from others; the love of the Father manifested in the Son is communicated to each by the mediation of others. Everyone remains attentive to the others, who are the manifestation of Jesus Christ. This unity proceeds from the willingness faithfully to receive from and to give attention to others.

The light of Christ does not come to us from others as an echo of our own thoughts; it comes in alien guise and speaks with a foreign accent, and it shatters the barricades of our selves, leaving us open to others so that Christ's light can pass through us to others. Christ's light —which is a metaphor for the Father's love manifest in Christ—creates unity by enabling us to love those who are not ourselves and do not resemble ourselves, to love them although and because they are immutably other. This unity arises from a twofold shattering of boundaries—the boundaries that separate us from the Father's will and from each other—and from a twofold fidelity—to the Father and to each other. It is a unity born of the transmission of love, whose origin is the Father, and human leaders can only be agents or catalysts or guides in its achievement.

To know Jesus is to recognize him as a missionary. So Jesus himself told the disciples: "Now they know that all thy gifts have come to me from thee; for I have taught them all that I learned from thee, and they have received it: they know with certainty that I came from thee; they have had faith to believe that thou didst send me" (John 17:7–8).

2

"The world did not recognize him"

HE KNEW ALL OF THEM

The mission will not be a triumphal march. Should it be received with enthusiasm, the missionary will know that this enthusiasm is superficial or misconceived, because the world does not know either the Father or the one sent from the Father. The mission must overcome not only cultural barriers but the world's total ignorance.

In John's language the world is people, and the Jews represent all people. Jesus' rejection by the Jews signified his rejection by the world, that is, all people. John's story of the conflict between Jesus and the Jews is in fact a metaphor for the real drama of humanity: It was a particular episode of history, but it embodied what happened and will happen in all generations and in all peoples.

One knows the world only by knowing the Father. Therefore those who know not the Father or the Son do not know themselves either. The Jews did not know their own hearts.

They judged themselves pious and religious because of their carnal bond with Abraham that led, presumably, to their spiritual bond with his merits. "Abraham is our father" (8:39). They considered themselves children of God because they were proprietors of God's words, and this ownership hid the real impiety behind the religious self-deception: "We are not base-born; God is our father, and God alone" (8:41). But Jesus saw them—and in them all of us—for what they were: "Your father is the devil and you choose to carry out your father's desires" (8:44).

Every culture is an interpretation of reality, and a major part of every culture's interpretation is a falsification of reality, to protect its members from truths they do not wish to know or have known. Individuals as well as groups expend much of their psychological energy elaborating ideologies, or facades, to shield their real selves from others' eyes—and from their own. This self-defense is composed of lies, the greatest of which are those that people tell themselves to secure their own tranquility.

Scientific and philosophic criticism has slowly and with difficulty uncovered some of those illusions that people create for themselves in order to hide, and hide from, their reality; but Jesus unmasked them completely and immediately. The Jews, meaning the world, are children of the devil because "he is a liar and the father of lies" (8:44), and they live lies in order to be comfortable and secure.

We are all the same. We elaborate reasons, motives, justifications to hide, from others and ourselves, our own cowardice, disloyalty, and lack of love. Likewise, peoples, societies, classes, and governments create ideologies in order to defend and justify injustice, domination, and exploitation of others. Needless to say, these lies are spontaneous and unconscious. Those who live a lie cannot perceive it; they believe themselves to be "children of Abraham" or "children of God." To perceive one's own lie, one must be already in the way of salvation. The consciousness of innocence is the very clearest manifestation of the lie in the soul.

Having been sent by the Father from heaven, Jesus was not deceived by human pretenses or by demonstrations of popular enthusiasm. "But Jesus for his part would not trust himself to them. He knew men so well, all of them, that he needed no evidence from others about a man, for he himself could tell what was in a man" (2:24–25).

Various episodes in the Gospel demonstrate Jesus' knowledge of the world. He was unperturbed by the common-sense challenge of the Pharisee Nicodemus, because he knew that this common sense masked an ignorance of the essential. "Is this famous teacher of Israel ignorant of such things?" (3:10). Nicodemus himself did not know that he was ignorant. To the Jews, outraged because he healed and the healed man carried off his pallet on the Sabbath, Jesus replied, "with you it is different, as I know well, for you have no love for God in you" (5:42).

The miracle of loaves and fishes roused the crowd to enthusiasm, but Jesus knew the superficiality of this reaction. "I know that you have not come looking for me because you saw signs, but because you ate the bread and your hunger was satisfied" (6:26). Then came the discourse explaining the signs, and the disciples began to murmur. "Jesus was aware that his disciples were murmuring about it and asked them, 'Does this shock you? . . . The words which I have spoken to you are both spirit and life. And yet there are some of you who have no faith' " (6:61–64). The Evangelist adds: "For Jesus knew all along who were

without faith and who was to betray him"
(6:64).

In fact, Jesus said to the Twelve: " 'Have I
not chosen you, all twelve? Yet one of you is a
devil.' He meant Judas, son of Simon Iscariot.
He it was who would betray him, and he was
one of the Twelve" (6:70–71). He told the Jews
that they wanted to kill him before they themselves were conscious of their intentions:
"When you have lifted up the Son of man . . ."
(8:28); "I know that you are descended from
Abraham, but you are bent on killing me because my teaching makes no headway with
you" (8:37).

HIS OWN WOULD NOT RECEIVE HIM

"The light shines on in the dark" (1:5). The
world remained in darkness, although the presence of the light revealed the darkness for
what it was: ignorance and untruth. By speaking plain truth, Jesus exposed ideologies as
self-serving falsehoods, but the world refused
to see. The Fourth Gospel points out with con-
spicuous insistence the incomprehension of
the Jews, not so as to condemn the Jews alone,
but by them to exemplify humankind. If the
Jews, who had received the sacred Scriptures,
could be so uncomprehending, how much
blinder the rest of the world must be!

The world does not see or understand or per-

ceive its own failure to see or understand. The
blank incomprehension that Jesus encountered revealed the falseness of all contemporary religions. Of true knowledge of God there
was none, but the manifold misconceptions of
God allowed people to feel tranquil and secure
in the belief that they knew him and were
doing his will.

None of us can feel safe from this danger.
Christianity is equally susceptible to perver-
sion into a human defense mechanism against
the true God; our cult of Jesus can be a wall
that we build, individually and collectively, to
avoid the impact of the true Christ. The Jews
invoked God in order to defend themselves
against the true presence of God, and we may
invoke Jesus in the same way. The Fourth
Gospel supplies real-life examples of the
blindness and ignorance described in Mat-
thew: "Lord, when was it that we saw you
hungry or thirsty or a stranger or naked or ill
or in prison, and did nothing for you?" (Matt.
25:44).

Jesus' opponents were not common crimi-
nals, well-known reprobates, public delin-
quents. Quite the contrary, they were the pil-
lars of the community, honorable people, re-
spected and respectable. They did not reject
Jesus or abuse him because they were base,
ignorant, and immoral by community stan-
dards, but precisely because they were the

acknowledged estimable, learned, and virtuous members of the community. Their objections proceeded not from social weakness but from social strength mobilized to defend their false ideology and egotism.

"There was one of the Pharisees named Nicodemus, a member of the Jewish Council" (3:1). But his wisdom faltered against Jesus' first words. When Nicodemus asked, "How is this possible?" (3:9), Jesus replied: To understand me you must abandon the conventional wisdom and disregard public opinion. But Nicodemus feared the unforeseeable consequences of such unorthodoxy and preferred not to understand.

Jesus' expulsion of the money-changers and animal-dealers from the temple precincts likewise puzzled the community. Such an action did not fall within their conception of religion. They asked Jesus his authority for such an act (2:18) and, having failed to understand the act, failed also to understand his answer. His performing cures on the Sabbath scandalized them equally (5:16; 9:16). Finally, his raising of Lazarus determined them to seek his death. They could understand it only in political terms, and in those terms it was potentially disastrous (chap. 11).

The Pharisees were not hypocrites. They were not pretending, for their own advantage, not to understand. They really did not understand; they could not. And they could not because their culture and personalities contained no category for Jesus' way of being.

The eighth chapter is a long dialogue between Jesus and the Pharisees, but it is a dialogue revealing the impossibility of a dialogue between them. The Pharisees cannot and will not understand. "The Pharisees said to him, 'You are witness in your own cause; your testimony is not valid' " (8:13); "Where is your father?" (8:19), and finally, after all Jesus had told them, they asked, "Who are you?" (8:25). To have understood would have required destroying totally a system on which their personal equilibrium and the equilibrium of their society was based.

For this inability to understand, Jesus had no remedy. The more he explained, the less the Pharisees understood.

> This testimony to me was given by the Father who sent me, although you never heard his voice, or saw his form. But his word has found no home in you, for you do not believe the one whom he sent (5: 37–38).
>
> I have come accredited by my Father, and you have no welcome for me; if another comes self-accredited you will welcome him (5:43).

How could the Pharisees have more confidence in a person who came in his own name than in one sent from God? Simply because a person like themselves would not threaten their beliefs or way of life. He would speak their language; they would recognize in him their own thoughts. They might disagree on details but not on major principles, and their categories of thought would be identical. Jesus not only contradicted their principles, he obliterated their whole ideology.

"You do not know either where I came from or where I am going" (8:14). "You know neither me nor my Father" (8:19). "Why do you not understand my language? It is because my revelation is beyond your grasp" (8:43). Jesus spoke to them of the pastor and of the sheep, but "they did not understand what he meant by it" (10:6). Not comprehending Jesus the man, they certainly could not afterward comprehend the Spirit of truth, whom the world cannot receive, "because the world neither sees nor knows him" (14:17). Wanting to kill Jesus, they would be even more zealous afterward to kill his followers: "The time is coming when anyone who kills you will suppose that he is performing a religious duty. They will do these things because they do not know either the Father or me" (16:2–3).

Jesus' whole experience of the world could be

condensed into his prayer at the Last Supper: "O righteous Father, ... the world does not know thee" (17:25). The world's ignorance, its inability to understand, was so profound that they who were children of the devil (8:44) sincerely accused Jesus of harboring a devil: "Are we not right in saying that you are a Samaritan, and that you are possessed?" (8:48). "Now we are certain that you are possessed" (8:52).

The world's incomprehension is not merely intellectual. It is a complete rejection, a willingness to expel from society, from humanity itself, the alien presence that disturbs and unsettles it. The Jews did not perceive this at once, but Jesus did: He knew from the beginning that they could not but will his death. Therefore any church or message or gospel that encounters much wordly success—much welcome, favor, and honor in the world—must be automatically suspect. If people receive us thus, could it be because our words only repeat the false reasonings and ideologies that reinforce their security and tranquillity by making injustice seem the most perfect justice?

By no stretch of interpretation does the Fourth Gospel blame certain individuals for Jesus' death; on the contrary, the Evangelist attributes that death to the world's opposition to God: "This made the Jews still more determined to kill him, because he was not only breaking the Sabbath, but by calling God his own Father, he claimed equality with God" (5:18). "Afterwards Jesus went about in Galilee. He wished to avoid Judaea because the Jews were looking for a chance to kill him" (7:1). Later he went up to the temple for a feast and asked the Jews: " 'Why are you trying to kill me?' The crowd answered, 'You are possessed! Who wants to kill you?' " (7:20).

The people did not know, but some in the midst of the people knew and were amazed that the authorities allowed him to continue to speak: "Is not this the man they want to put to death? And here he is, speaking openly, and they have not a word to say to him. Can it be that our rulers have actually decided that this is the Messiah?" (7:25–27). Such was hardly the case: "The chief priests and the Pharisees sent temple police to arrest him" (7:32), but these refrained from seizing him because it appeared that some of the people would defend him (7:42–44). John explains, "No one arrested him, because his hour had not yet come" (8:20), but from this time on Jesus' discourses increasingly inflamed the fear and anger of the community: "They picked up stones to throw at him, but Jesus was not to be seen; and he left the temple" (8:59).

Finally his hour came. The raising of Lazarus sealed Jesus' death, and the leaders of the people looked for an opportunity to apprehend him. Thereupon, according to the

Evangelist, signs of the approaching hour multiplied (11:47–57; 12:7, 9–11,27–28,31–36; 13: 1,21–30). The Evangelist's account of the passion and death show the leaders of the people, the Pharisees and the priests, relentlessly following Jesus, pressing the Roman governor to deliver him over to death on the cross.

The narration of the passion clarifies the opposition, the incompatibility, and the conflict between the one sent from the Father and the world: "The world, though it owed its being to him, did not recognize him" (1:10).

The community leaders, the Pharisees and priests, were clear and united on the need for Jesus' death, but the common people, John makes clear, were uncertain, confused, and divided in their opinions (7:12,43). Their naive enthusiasm to proclaim Jesus king (6:15), which had been aroused by the miracles, lapsed into perplexity and wavering: "There was much whispering about him in the crowds. 'He is a good man,' said some. 'No,' said others, 'he is leading the people astray.' However, no one talked about him openly, for fear of the Jews" (7:12–13). While some people said, "This must certainly be the expected prophet!" or "This is the Messiah," others argued that "surely the Messiah is not to come from Galilee. Does not Scripture say that the Messiah is to be of the family of David, from David's village of Bethlehem?' Thus he caused a split among the people" (7:41–43).

When Jesus went up to Jerusalem for the last Passover, a great crowd, awed by news of the raising of Lazarus, went out to meet him and accompany him into the city (12:12–19). But when Jesus was apprehended, they made no protest; indeed, they were nowhere in evidence. They were not deliberate persecutors, but they trembled before the authorities. Just as the historical leaders who willed Jesus' death also symbolize all people who resist God, so the common people who flocked to him and then deserted him symbolize the world's cowardice-born complicity in crime.

The apostles too symbolize an aspect of the world. Even they balked at understanding Jesus' most profound, radical, and metaphorically couched discourses: "This is more than we can stomach! Why listen to such talk?" (6:60). It is true that when Jesus was going to face almost certain death, Thomas said to the other disciples, "Let us also go, that we may die with him" (11:16). But when Jesus was actually taken, all save two fled, and of these two, Peter later denied him out of fear.

THE POWER OF DARKNESS

What was the reason for the world's incomprehension, its failure to recognize Jesus, the one sent from the Father? Why did the Jews—who symbolize all the peoples of the earth—reject Jesus? This question is one of the principal themes of the Fourth Gospel, and one to which Jesus himself gave diverse, but complementary and convergent, answers. One who is in himself light and lives in the light goes to the light, he said; one who is darkness and lives in the darkness prefers darkness and flees the light (3:20–21). This means that those who share the nature of the Son and the Father recognize themselves in Jesus and go to him, and those who lack love find Jesus alien and antipathetic. The world, lacking love, is not missionary, is not a link in the transmission of love, and therefore is unable to recognize Jesus. The world, in fact, is the complete opposite of the Son: It lives for itself and seeks its salvation in itself. Seeking there its salvation, it is lost.

Jesus told this first to Nicodemus: "Flesh can give birth only to flesh; it is spirit that gives birth to spirit. You ought not to be astonished then, when I tell you that you must be born over again" (3:6–7). John the Baptist, speaking of Jesus to his own disciples, put the same thought into other images (3:31). What do these images signify? To understand him who comes from "above," from the "Spirit," it is necessary to be of the same nature, and the world is not of the Spirit, therefore not of the same nature as Jesus.

Here lies the test; the light has come into the world, but men preferred dark-

ness to light because their deeds were evil.
Bad men all hate the light and avoid it, for
fear their practices should be shown up.
The honest man comes to the light so that
it may be clearly seen that God is in all he
does (3:19–21).

The "evil deeds" of those who love darkness
are the converse of Jesus' works; they also express unbelief in and rejection of Jesus. Faith
in and knowledge of Jesus are in all the deeds
of those who "come to the light." Whoever goes
to Jesus does so by virtue of connaturality, of a
radical likeness in being. Whoever flees from
him shows thereby that his being is funda-
mentally incompatible with Jesus' being. Such
people are the converse of mission and missionary; they are creatures isolated in their
separate egocentrisms.

The great polemic of the eighth chapter de-
velops these themes: "You belong to this world
below, I to the world above. Your home is in
this world, mine is not" (8:23). The statement is
not literal but metaphorical; the reference is
not to separate places of origin but to antithetical ways of being.

To belong to the world is to be the devil's
progeny, and as in Chapter 1 of Genesis the
devil is death and lies and brings death by
means of lies. Jesus said to them:

Your father is the devil and you choose
to carry out your father's desires. He was

a murderer from the beginning, and is not rooted in the truth; there is no truth in him. When he tells a lie he is speaking his own language, for he is a liar and the father of lies. But I speak the truth and therefore you do not believe me. . . . He who has God for his father listens to the words of God. You are not God's children; that is why you do not listen (8:44–47).

Whoever belongs to the world also lies, that is, rejects the truth, and rejecting the truth makes one a murderer, indirectly if not directly. The whole Gospel illustrates how one may be concretely guilty of murder without being the immediate cause of death.

REMAINING IN THE WORLD

The opposition between Jesus and the world is a permanent dimension of history. "If the world hates you, it hated me first, as you know well. If you belonged to the world, the world would love its own; but because you do not belong to the world, because I have chosen you out of the world, for that reason the world hates you" (15:18–19). Only the existence of the mission makes the world conscious of being "world," that is, of being different from God. The persecution of the disciples reiterated Jesus' persecution and death. Missionaries

who have since then continued the presence
and the way of being of the risen Son reveal by
contrast the evil of the world and, like Jesus,
provoke division among people.

Not every theological division or disagree-
ment, however, accurately reflects opposition
between God and the world. The nature of this
opposition has been often and variously mis-
construed.

Completely alien to the Gospel, for example,
would be an opposition between Jesus as immaterial reality and the world as material reality, with salvation defined as denying the
material and taking refuge in the immaterial.
In the New Testament, Spirit does not mean
immateriality, but life, dynamism, love, communication.

It is even less valid to identify the world with
human society and God with the monastic or
eremitic life. Evil is not the necessary con-
comitant of human society or history nor is
good an inevitable attribute of solitude. On the
contrary, Jesus lived his whole mission sur-
rounded by people.

Finally, the world must not be confused with
civil or lay society and God, in contrast, identified with the institutional church. The opposition between God and the world has nothing
to do with the traditional rivalry between
church and state.

Christ and the world represent, respectively, openness to God's way of being and to Christ's mission, and lack of love and total egocentrism (individual or collective). The world is the antithesis of mission, but it is not identified with a particular or predestined group of people. No one pertains to this world by nature. People can pass from the world to the category of disciples, from darkness to light. Mission does not divide the immutably good from the irretrievably evil. Mission is manifestly good. It reveals, by contrast, what is evil. By revealing the difference between good and evil, it requires people to choose. What mission does, in other words, is mandate our choice between good and evil.

> If I had not come and spoken to them, they would not be guilty of sin; but now they have no excuse for their sin. . . . If I had not worked among them and accomplished what no other man has done, they would not be guilty of sin; but now they have both seen and hated both me and my Father (15:22–24).

The mission is not to reject this world, to condemn it, to proclaim God's wrath, or to implement it. It is to free the world from its ignorance of the Father, from its unbelief and unwillingness to believe, from its lie, its death.

It is to save the world by revealing the choice between good and evil.

How, in the concrete events and situations of human history, are missionaries to reveal this choice?

3

"The Word made flesh"

JESUS' WORKS

The one sent by God was made flesh, says the prologue of John's Gospel. This "incarnation" does not signify only what happened in the moment of conception. For the coming of the Son "in the flesh" is a permanent operation. The "Word became flesh" and was incarnate in every moment of Jesus' life. As the Council of Chalcedon points out, "incarnation" expresses the union of two natures in one person. John, however, defines "the incarnation" in concrete detail. What is incarnated is the Father's word, his dynamism, his active, transmitted love. All this becomes incarnate, becomes human, in Jesus, the one whom the Father sent. The "flesh" is the human being who lives and acts, the person as "worker." Since work is a God-ordained human activity, John has defined the incarnation as God's dynamism entering into and animating Jesus' human capacity for work.

What is work? It is to use all one's human powers, mental and corporal, to transform the world. To do this, one must transform individuals, culture, and nature, not by decree, or by magic, or by prayerfully leaving things to God, but by human effort. That is what Jesus came to do.

Missionaries are neither philosophers, professors, preachers, nor propagandists for any cause whatever. They are not content with ideas, intentions, words, symbolic gestures. Missionaries are workers, and workers seek results. It is no accident that the Fourth Gospel de-emphasized doctrine and creed. Jesus was not a doctor of laws. The doctors of laws dealt in words: They interpreted, commented, expounded—and they changed nothing. Jesus worked to transform people. The Evangelist's contrast between words and work, though implicit, could hardly be more emphatic. Let us examine first the theme of work in the Fourth Gospel and then the examples of works that illustrate the theme.

"It is meat and drink for me to do the will of him who sent me until I have finished his work" (4:34). To explain his cure of the paralytic on the Sabbath, Jesus invoked the same reason: "My Father has never yet ceased his work, and I am working too" (5:17). The work of the one sent is the work of the Father, the work given to him by the Father, the real work of the Father.

> The Son can do nothing by himself; he does only what he sees the Father doing: what the Father does, the Son does. For the Father loves the Son and shows him all his works, and will show greater yet, to fill you with wonder. As the Father raises the dead and gives them life, so the Son gives life to men, as he determines (5:19–21).

Here for the first time is stated the object of the work: to give life.

The cure of the paralytic gave Jesus the opportunity to explain the Father's works. In the same way the cure of the man born blind allowed him to reiterate and expand the explanation.

> As he went on his way Jesus saw a man blind from his birth. His disciples put the questions, "Rabbi, who sinned, this man or his parents? Why was he born blind?" "It is not that this man or his parents sinned," Jesus answered; "he was born blind so that God's power might be displayed in curing him. While daylight lasts we must carry on the work of him who sent

me; night comes, when no one can work.
While I am in the world I am the light of
the world." With these words he spat on
the ground . . . (9:1–6).

To work is to illuminate, to restore vision to
those who do not see.

In response to the accusations of the
Pharisees, Jesus cited his works, not doctrines
or titles.

My deeds done in my Father's name are
my credentials" (10:25).

I have set before you many good deeds,
done by my Father's power; for which of
these would you stone me? (10:32).

If I am not acting as my Father would,
do not believe me. But if I am, accept the
evidence of my deeds, even if you do not
believe me, so that you may recognize and
know that the Father is in me and I in the
Father (10:37–39).

In his final prayer Jesus presented his entire
life to the Father: "I have glorified thee on
earth by completing the work which thou
gavest me to do" (17:4).

The Gospel describes for us some of Jesus'
works—Jesus at Cana, with Nicodemus, with
the official at Capernaum, with the Samaritans, with the paralytic, with the Galileans at

the sea of Tiberias, with the Jews in the temple
at Jerusalem, with the man born blind, with
Lazarus and his sisters. John narrates these
works in order to show us how Jesus worked.

Superficially his works reveal Jesus sometimes as teacher, sometimes as preacher,
sometimes as miracle-worker. But in all of
them his true intent was to transform people:
to help them pass through abandonment, misery, sin, darkness, and death to light and life.
To accomplish this transformation, he was
willing to do whatever was necessary.

Sometimes, of course, his utmost efforts
failed: Nicodemus, the Samaritans, the Galileans, and the Pharisees could not, because
they would not, understand, and therefore
could not be transformed.

We must understand that Jesus, in performing his miracles, aimed not only at the cure of
bodily misery, but beyond that to the passage
of the person from a state of darkness and
death to a state of life. The intended end of
Jesus' cures was a renewed person, one who
was saved, liberated from the world to live in
truth, capable of a new existence. Now, however, let us return from the ultimate purpose
of the works to the nature of the work itself.

Jesus' work is in fact a combat—against evil
and against all the social forces that preserve
and foster evil. Jesus had to fight not only
against evil, but against all the people who

wanted to prohibit him from fighting evil. His weapons were words and "signs," employed separately or together as the situation required, but employed always for the same end: humanity's liberation from evil and rebirth in truth.

THE SIGNS

One element of Jesus' work, then, was signs. These were visible material or corporeal transformations intended to begin and signify some person's passage from darkness to light. Jesus found signs necessary to engage people's attention, but not all of those who accepted the signs as godly understood them to be signposts to total conversion and renewal. For some, in fact, the signs were counterproductive, leading no further than naive acceptance of and dependence on the wonder-working capacities of Jesus. We cannot emphasize too strongly that Jesus did not come to resolve human problems by means of miracles. As mere miracle-worker, his only achievements would have been a cult (with shrines and pilgrimages) to himself and a following comfortably convinced that they could rely completely on him to order their lives aright. Jesus' purpose was diametrically opposite. His miracles, in themselves extraordinary acts of charity, were also symbols of renewal and a means to open people's eyes to the choice between good and evil that must be made by them.

The first sign John records is the miracle at Cana: "This deed at Cana-in-Galilee is the first of the signs by which Jesus revealed his glory and led his disciples to believe in him" (2:11). The second was the healing of the official's son (4:54). After these came the miracle of the loaves and fishes, the cure of the paralytic and the man congenitally blind, and the raising of Lazarus. John tells us that there were many more signs; he has not recorded them all, but the disciples witnessed them (20:30). The Fourth Gospel gives the impression of a multitude of miracles on behalf of the miserable and the infirm: "A large crowd of people followed who had seen the signs he performed in healing the sick" (6:2).

Seeing the signs "led his disciples to believe in him" (2:11), but the majority of the people were not convinced by the signs: "In spite of the many signs which Jesus had performed in their presence they would not believe in him" (12:37). The signs could capture people's attention; to those with eyes to see, they could indicate what was evil in the world; but not everyone had eyes to see.

Even among these convinced by the signs there were degrees of belief. "Many gave their allegiance to him when they saw the signs that he performed" (2:23), but "Jesus for his part would not trust himself to them. He knew men so well, all of them . . ." (2:24). "Rabbi," said Nicodemus, "we know that you are a teacher sent by God; no one could perform these signs of yours unless God were with him" (3:2), but though he believed in the miracles, he did not understand Jesus' message. The crowd that experienced the miracle of the loaves and fishes was impressed enough to want to make Jesus king: "Surely this must be the prophet that was to come into the world" (6:14), but Jesus recognized that "you have not come looking for me because you saw signs, but because you ate the bread and your hunger was satisfied" (6:26).

The signs can open the way to faith, but for those who cannot see the meaning beneath the sign, they constitute as great an obstacle to faith as the Scriptures did for the Pharisees.

THE TEACHINGS

The second element of Jesus' work was his words. These too merit the name of work; they were works, not rhetoric. Jesus did not give courses in religion or philosophy. His discourses were tools of persuasion, for his purpose was the conversion of the world, which can be obtained neither by violence nor by seduction but only by persuasion. John's purpose in narrating Jesus' discourses is to convey an image of Jesus' work.

Jesus spoke, or taught (they were one and the same) in all circumstances—in the synagogue of Capernaum (6:59), in the temple (7:14), on the shore of Lake Tiberias (6:25–40), to multitudes or to one man "by night" (3:2). His discourses were in effect commentaries on his signs, attempts to explain that the literal signs symbolized and called for human renewal. At the same time, however, his discourses contained God's word that he had been sent to communicate and were therefore a co-equal part of his mission, not mere footnotes to the signs. Through his brief ministry Jesus reiterated this: "I do not speak on my own authority, but the Father who sent me has himself commanded me what to say and how to speak. . . . What the Father has said to me, therefore—that is what I speak" (12:49,50).

"The teaching that I give is not my own; it is the teaching of him who sent me" (7:16). When he knew his hour to be at hand, he reported on the mission to his Father: "I have taught them all that I learned from thee, and they have received it: they knew with certainty that I came from thee; they have had faith to believe that thou didst send me" (17:8), and "I have delivered thy word to them" (17:14).

The Father's words are not words in the lit-

eral sense, however. They are not words about
God or about religion. God did not send Jesus to
teach a catechism or a catalogue of dogmas or
a theology to humanity. The Father's word
was its content: God's love and openness to
humanity, expressed and communicated to us
by Jesus' mission. Jesus had to translate his
love and openness into human vocabulary. He
had to find the words and images that could
transmit the conviction that God speaks and is
open to humanity. It is the common task of all
missionaries.

In Jesus' mission to speak is to do and to do is
to speak. The work was the words, and the
words were the work. His meaning transcends
the common and customary meaning of the
words he used; nevertheless, it could be understood. God's word is not perfectly expressible
in any human language, yet Jesus, using ordinary human language, expressed and transmitted it. That was his work: to transform
words so that they could transmit the word of
the Father.

THE TESTIMONY OF THE WORKS

Jesus' works were doubly efficacious: They
transformed and saved the people to whom
they were applied and simultaneously served
as testimony to the people who were present at
the transformation. What they accomplished
in a single beneficiary they initiated in many

onlookers. That is why all missionary action must be open and public. Nothing could be more alien to Jesus' mission than the private cultivation of a disciple by a teacher. Missionaries must not only save; their saving works must testify to their mission, and that they can do only in public.

There is enough to testify that the Father has sent me, in the works my Father gave me to do (5:36).

If I am not acting as my Father would, do not believe me. But if I am, accept the evidence of my deeds, even if you do not believe me, so that you may recognize and know that the Father is in me and I in the Father (10:37–38).

Do you not believe that I am in the Father, and the Father in me? I am not myself the source of the words I speak to you: it is the Father who dwells in me doing his own work. Believe me when I say that I am in the Father and the Father in me; or else accept the evidence of the deeds themselves (14:10–11).

THE GREATER WORKS
OF THE MISSIONARIES

Jesus' work is also the work of the disciples sent by him: "In truth, in very truth I tell you, he who has faith in me will do what I am doing;

and he will do greater things still" (14:12). Jesus was not referring to the performance of physical miracles, but to the awakening of people to faith and life. This the apostles did and, as Jesus had predicted and we can see in Acts, they awakened and transformed a greater number of people than he himself had done. Let us see how the disciples' works were a continuation of the works of Jesus.

Obviously the Gospels contain no instruction manual for missionary activity. God's word, as we have said, did not come as a set of instructions but as Jesus himself. Therefore all missionaries must determine their own methods, suiting words and action to circumstances. Within this necessity for individual decision and initiative lies the possibility of error and corruption.

The forms and structures of behavior of every society powerfully influence its members' actions, the more so as its members are generally unaware of such influence. These forms and structures have their own dynamism that tends toward certain results regardless of the explicit intentions of the person acting. True human freedom of action is limited and difficult to achieve; it requires careful analysis and profound understanding of society's established modes and structures, so that one can modify these according to circumstances to achieve one's true ends. Since mission by definition takes place within human society, it, like any human enterprise, is always powerfully subject to the transforming or perverting influence of the very world it seeks to transform.

History is full of examples. The apostles had to find in their social contexts the forms of their social action. Often the dynamism of these forms caused them to diverge, quite unconsciously, from the work of Jesus Christ. The established forms of behavior subtly pervaded and perverted their activity so as to destroy the leaven, or saving efficacy, of the Gospel. Maurras, who feared the Gospel leaven as a breeder of social disorders and of anarchy, praised the Roman church for extirpating it.

The church took the priesthood of the Roman world as its model, and it transformed its ministers into administrators of a cult, performers of rites, perpetuators of tradition, teachers of doctrines about an invisible world, magistrates of social deportment. From fishers of men, which Jesus had bade them be, they became functionaries of religion.

During the Reformation the priestly role was somewhat remodelled by both Protestants and Catholics. "Pastors" came to resemble the doctors of the law of the ancient synagogue. They were proprietors of the Bible, custodians and sole authorized interpreters of the sacred words, and, as such, wellsprings and guard-

ians of private, familial, and social morality
and of intellectual orthodoxy as well. From
fishers of men, which Jesus intended them to
be, they had become prisoners of the Book, of
the law, of the order that must be maintained.
Captives of their own authority, how could
they be free to imitate Jesus?

To carry on Jesus' work, missionaries must
preserve their freedom. They must be free not
only of the honors, privileges, aggrandize-
ments, and satisfactions that society confers
on its disciplined and faithful functionaries,
but also of the functions themselves. The roles
that society seeks to impose on its religious
functionaries serve to buttress society, not to
transform it; they cannot but be antithetical
to Jesus' mission. Society's approbation is the
clearest sign of the missionary's failure. True
missionaries are always "outsiders" in their
societies and "ahead of their times." They take
their cues for action, not from established customs and conventional wisdom, but from their
own sincere, disinterested meditations on
Jesus' words and signs; and they judge their
actions, not by society's approval, but by the
Gospel's intent.

The missionary must first of all understand
the meaning of the signs. They were not tes-
timonials to Jesus' divinity but manifestations
of the Father's presence. They were not demonstrations of the Father's power but of his

love. The signs were acts of resurrection and
life that delivered people from weakness and
evil to strength and good. The signs show that
God speaks to us and that his word is life.

In the Acts of the Apostles Peter summarized Jesus' missionary work: "You know
about Jesus of Nazareth, how God anointed
him with the Holy Spirit and with power. He
went about doing good and healing all who
were oppressed by the devil" (Acts 10:38). The
Spirit is the strength to do good. The missionaries' work is to use all their strength and
faculty to do good. Faithful administration of
teaching of dogmas or precepts does not manifest the reality of the Father. Doing good
manifests the Father's reality.

Doing good cannot be a preplanned activity
rationally directed to the achievement of a
specific objective; it produces material or obvious results only sometimes and, as it were,
incidentally. It is, rather, action that continues the current of love communicated from
the Father to Jesus and from Jesus to all who
recognized him. Its purpose is simply to
awaken people to the Father's love, to transmit the force of the Spirit into the world. Thus,
though it appears in worldly terms a gratui-
tous and inefficacious activity, the object of
doing good is nothing less than to change the
world.

The mission cannot achieve the redemption

of the world, however; it can only begin it, only sow the seed in humanity. The signs were a beginning, but the concrete good they did was minuscule compared to the world's amplitude of evil—a handful fed out of millions hungry, a handful healed out of millions sick. Mission does not consist in bringing complete salvation to humanity. Although Jesus substituted himself for humanity in the mystery of the cross, he did not do so in the daily struggle to live a new life. The resurrection of the world to a new life is not the responsibility of any one missionary but the task of all people in every generation.

The messianic hope of a redemption accomplished once and for all by one messiah is a false hope but a seductive one. People want saviors, but woe to any who accept such a role. Either the world crushes them, as it did Jesus for threatening its established order, or it first enthrones them and then crushes them for failing of their promise. Missionaries must remember that Jesus denied messiahship throughout his ministry. One person, even if he could maintain his reputation as messiah throughout his own life, could not possibly establish a lasting new world. A new world must be accomplished by us; it cannot be accomplished for us by an individual savior.

To acknowledge these limitations, however, is not to excuse a missionary's inadequacy or justify failure or adduce the uselessness of missionary activity. Our purpose is to turn people away from mistaken hopes in a messiah to true understanding of the purpose of the signs and a genuine responsibility for their own salvation.

Just as missionaries must understand the significance of the signs, they must also understand the proper function of words. The words of mission are neither catechism nor sacred history nor code of laws or ethics that the missionaries must teach. They are a means toward twin ends (which are ultimately identical): to convey to human understanding the Word, which is the Father's love and openness, and to explain the signs. The missionaries' job is to formulate the discourses that will accomplish these twin purposes, remembering the while that their strength lies, not in their own eloquence, but in the Father's authority and the value of the works.

Words are the missionaries' weapons against the world, and their whole strength derives from their fidelity to the Word. Neither state backing nor clerical wealth nor intellectual prestige can enhance them. Quite the contrary, in fact, for none of these can communicate love or open souls to God.

We have spoken of the missionary's "job," but the mission is not an economic or social function. No one is a missionary for the working day only or, conversely, as an avocation. Mission entails the missionary's whole life and presence in the world. In this way mission "became flesh" in Jesus and made visible the glory of the Son of God.

4

"We saw his glory"

GLORY

"The word became flesh; he came to dwell among us, and we saw his glory, such glory as befits the Father's only Son, full of grace and truth" (1:14).

The summation and quintessence of Jesus' works was his incarnation, in which his glory was manifest. For his works, as we have said, signified little in themselves; their whole significance lay in the glory they communicated. In speaking of Jesus as the one sent, the one who was simultaneously the Father's messenger and his message to the world (Chapter 1), we dealt implicitly with the Father's glory as it was communicated by the mission. Now we must examine and define this glory explicitly.

The English word "glory," in its common

meanings, is a traditional but most inadequate translation of the original Hebrew, for which there are no European equivalents, not even in Greek or Latin. Jesus' works revealed his greatness, his force, his amplitude, his power, but with no suggestion of the potential domination of others connoted by these words. "Glory" is probably the best available word, provided we take it to mean, not "fame" or "grandeur" (which are extrinsic attributes), but transcendent goodness or holiness (which is an intrinsic attribute). If Jesus' glory had consisted of pomp, splendor, or renown, it would hardly have been recognized by humble provincial artisans and fishermen and overlooked or flouted by the great ones of his time. Jesus' unchanging authentic self was his glory, and his works were done to reveal it.

We must remember that according to the Bible the body does not obscure the soul nor does matter hide the spirit; rather, the immaterial is manifested by the material. Spirit and matter, soul and body are not opposed, but harmonious and complementary. The biblical authors found it inconceivable that the spirit or soul should manifest itself without the body, differing diametrically in this from classical Greek philosophy as well as from the major Oriental philosophies and religions. Therefore Jesus' corporeality was not assumed in any way to hide his reality but rather to manifest it. We need not ignore the material realities of Jesus' works; on the contrary, we must study them more carefully. Christianity's most dangerous temptation has always been toward a pseudo-mystical religious sensibility that would divorce Jesus Christ from his historical, corporeal reality.

In sum, Jesus' works, done to reveal his glory, were accomplished in his historical, corporeal reality: "This deed at Cana-in-Galilee is the first of the signs by which Jesus revealed his glory and led his disciples to believe in him" (2:11). Jesus' glory pertains to a transcendent reality that cannot be wholly explained by discourses. Nevertheless, Jesus did speak to his disciples in order to awaken and strengthen their understanding and faith. It is legitimate and neccessary for us to study his words to achieve the same purpose in our generation. Faith does not consist in listing from memory or acclaiming Jesus' attributes. It does not consist in an intellectual acceptance of these attributes. But the intellectual understanding of Jesus' words is certainly an aid to faith that we must not disdain. For the glory was made flesh, and this flesh expressed itself partly in words. We can validly use words to express a real perception of the glory.

Let us consider the attributes that Jesus used to express his glory.

In the first place, Jesus' use of "I am" in

itself constitutes the affirmation of his most complete and tremendous attribute. God too speaks thus; in the Old Testament, the divine "I am" is a statement of sovereignty. Jesus presented himself in the same way with the assurance of one who is truth. In him there was no distinction between the words and the reality, between the facade and the reality, between the visible and the real. His words expressed the truth of himself as no ordinary person can.

Jesus' cure of the man born blind was not only act but also metaphor—a symbolic demonstration and affirmation that he himself is light to the world:

> I am the light of the world. No follower of mine shall wander in the dark; he shall have the light of life (8:12).
>
> While I am in the world I am the light of the world (9:5).
>
> The light is among you still, but not for long. Go on your way while you have the light, so that darkness may not overtake you. He who journeys in the dark does not know where he is going. While you have the light, trust to the light, so that you may become men of light (12:35–36).
>
> I have come into the world as light, so that no one who has faith in me should remain in darkness (12:46).

Jesus is not only the light but the way to the Father that the light illuminates: "I am the way; I am the truth and I am life; no one comes to the Father except by me" (14:6).

Light and way have one purpose: They lead people to God. Similarly, the door admits people to God's presence and the shepherd leads them through it:

> I am the door of the sheepfold.... Anyone who comes into the fold through me shall be safe. He shall go in and out and shall find pastures (10:7–9).

> I am the good shepherd; ... the sheep hear his voice; he calls his own sheep by name, and leads them out. When he has brought them all out, he goes ahead and the sheep follow, because they know his voice (10:11,3–4).

The light, the way, the door, the shepherd are all metaphors for the truth. The truth that proceeded from the Father and was present in Jesus was the way Jesus encountered reality. Jesus said to the Jews:

> If you dwell within the revelation I have brought, you are indeed disciples; you shall know the truth, and the truth will set you free (8:31–32).

> But I speak the truth and therefore you do not believe me (8:45).

The truth leads to life, and Jesus used the word "life" after performing the sign of Lazarus: "I am the resurrection and I am life" (11:25). The sign of the multiplication of bread also suggests life: "I am the bread of life. Whoever comes to me shall never be hungry, and whoever believes in me shall never be thirsty" (6:35).

John summarizes the meaning of Jesus' glory: "Grace and truth came through Jesus Christ" (1:17). But the word "through" does not mean that Jesus was only a channel of transmission of God's salvation. He was grace and truth. That glory was in him. He led toward salvation, or "life," but he also was salvation. Not that he was the Father's rival, for he received that reality from the Father. Because he was the truth in its fullness, he was able to affirm, like God in the Old Testament: "In very truth I tell you, before Abraham was born, I am" (8:58). And the Jews understood very well the pretention that these words had, because they picked up stones to throw at him (8:59).

Jesus was the Father's grace in plenitude. Therefore John can say with certainty: "Out of his full store we have all received grace upon grace" (1:16). For "all that came to be was alive with his life, and that life was the light of men" (1:4). His glory was that the light was and is and will be in him. His works—the words that explain and the signs that show in the flesh the Spirit's truth—reveal that glory.

THE SON'S GLORY

Anyone whose teaching is merely his own, aims at honour for himself. But if a man aims at the honour of him who sent him he is sincere, and there is nothing false in him (7:18).

If I glorify myself, that glory of mine is worthless. It is the Father who glorifies me, he of whom you say, "He is our God" (8:54).

To glorify means to confer the glory, the value, the power, of which we speak.

Among people arise leaders, chiefs, heroes, and sages: Their glory is human honor and acclaim; it is a small glory, and deceptive at that, for people cannot confer true glory. Jesus' glory was not illusory, because it was not human in origin. Neither his mission nor his power came from himself, nor were they conferred by other people. Nothing was required from people. His glory was therefore immune to the fragility and disintegration of all human investitures: "I do not care about my own glory; there is one who does care, and he is judge" (8:50); "I do not look to men for honour" (5:41).

All Jesus' glory was the Father's gift. Jesus' works during his earthly life showed people the Father's own glory. This glory was in itself salvation, the gift of life, grace poured out upon the world; in its manifestation it was not mere spectacle of power but active benefi- cence. Therefore Jesus said to Martha: "Did I not tell you that if you have faith you will see the glory of God" (11:40). But faith was pre- cisely what the Jews would not have: "For they valued their reputation with men rather than the honour which comes from God" (12:43). Their fear of jeopardizing the illusory security of self-esteem and human approba- tion blinded them to God's manifest glory.

Jesus' glory was in him before the creation of the world and time: "Father, glorify me in thy own presence with the glory which I had with thee before the world began" (17:5). For "when all things began, the Word already was. The Word dwelt with God, and what God was, the Word was. . . . Through him all things came to be. . . . All that came to be was alive with his life" (1:1–4). In time (or human history), how- ever, the glory was clothed in flesh and en- tered the world: "We saw his glory" (1:14). And it was in human history, during his earthly existence, that Jesus received his first investi- ture: the first coming of the Spirit, which con- ferred God's glory upon him in the flesh. John the Baptist testified: "I saw the Spirit coming down from heaven like a dove and resting upon him. I did not know him, but he who sent me to baptize in water had told me, 'when you see the

Spirit coming down upon someone and resting upon him, you will know that this is he who is to baptize in the Holy Spirit' " (1:32–33). By virtue of this coming of the Spirit, Jesus was able to manifest his eternal glory in his earthly work.

Jesus' glory in the flesh was in turn only a precursor or prefigure of a greater glory. Only in the resurrection, after the passion and the cross, would Jesus be totally invested with the glory of the Son. John refers to this glorification of the Son in his comments on Jesus' words on the day of the feast of Tabernacles:

> Jesus stood and cried aloud, "If anyone is thirsty let him come to me; whoever believes in me, let him drink. As Scripture says, 'Streams of living water shall flow out from within him.' " He was speaking of the Spirit which believers in him would receive later; for the Spirit had not yet been given, because Jesus had not yet been glorified (7:37–39).

Death, as John speaks of it and as he reports Jesus speaking of it, was the entrance to glory. The glorification of the risen Jesus surpassed the glory manifested in his mortal life, as the works done after the Resurrection far surpassed those done before. Jesus and John spoke of death as if it were glorification itself.

Jesus' glorification was also by definition the glorification of the Father. Though God need not be invested with glory, since it is his originally and completely, his glory given to the Son was manifested with a new amplitude that was like a new glorification. A few days before his death Jesus said: " 'This hour has come for the Son of Man to be glorified. ... Now my soul is in turmoil, and what am I to say? Father, save me from this hour? No, it was for this that I came to this hour. Father, glorify thy name.' A voice sounded from heaven: 'I have glorified it, and I will glorify it again' " (12:23,27–28). And on his last night of mortal life, after Judas had left, Jesus said: "Now the Son of Man is glorified, and in him God is glorified. If God is glorified in him, God will also glorify him in himself; and he will glorify him now" (13:31–32).

The Father's glory, and therefore the Son's, was life in its optimum and maximum. In his own mortal life Jesus showed this power of life by means of his works, but they were only a token or figure of the life begun and shown in the exaltation on the cross and in the Resurrection. With the Resurrection the Son inaugurated a glory that will last until the final coming of the reign of God.

In his last prayer to the Father Jesus said:

Father, the hour has come. Glorify thy Son, that the Son may glorify thee. For

thou hast made him sovereign over all
mankind, to give eternal life to all whom
thou hast given him. This is eternal life: to
know thee who alone art truly God, and
Jesus Christ whom thou has sent. I have
glorified thee on earth by completing the
work which thou gavest me to do; and now,
Father, glorify me in thy own presence
with the glory which I had with thee before the world began (17:1–5).

The Son's glory was destined to be manifested by the works of his disciples—which
brings us to ourselves, for only we who are now
living can be his present disciples.

THE DISCIPLES' GLORY
AND WRETCHEDNESS

We have already cited the text in which
Jesus promised to the disciples greater works
than his own. Jesus' power will act in these
works, and by its action the Son will be
glorified and, with the Son, the Father: "In
truth, in very truth I tell you, he who has faith
in me will do what I am doing; and he will do
greater things still because I am going to the
Father. Indeed anything you ask in my name I
will do, so that the Father may be glorified in
the Son. If you ask anything in my name I will
do it" (14:12–14). The requests that Jesus
promises to answer refer to the apostles' fu-

ture works. Jesus was promising them his power to accomplish their works. His glory would be transmitted to them through the Spirit: "He will glorify me, for everything that he makes known to you he will draw from what is mine" (16:14).

On this level the Gospel is a great parable, explaining in human images and words the transmission and enlargement of Jesus' glory in human history. His power to do works and the glory manifested by the works were all passed on to the disciples.

Those sent by Jesus do not cease to be ordinary people. Their natures do not change. They partake of human weaknesses. Christian history leaves no doubt on this point. That is the extreme contradiction in which we live: While we are recipients of the glory that the Father gave the Son, we are simultaneously the world, human flesh immersed in the world. We have not yet transformed ourselves according to the Spirit's truth, yet we are already sent on the mission to realize the works of the Spirit.

Christianity is completely distinct from philosophy, human wisdom, or the practice of religion. Christians must communicate their experience of the Spirit. The tremendous immediacy of such personal communication can have a powerful impact on its recipients, but we must be sure that what we communicate is in fact the truth of the Spirit and not our private imaginings or public aspirations.

We bear a glory that is not ours. Insofar as possible we must submerge ourselves so that the glory can appear. We must remain always conscious of the ever-present distinction between the greatness of the gift we transmit and the insignificance and imperfections of we who transmit it. We carry a treasure of gold in vessels of clay.

The works that we do that manifest Christ's glory express one part of us. All of us do some evil; none of us is completely inspired by the Spirit to carry out the Father's work. People have a tendency to define others (and themselves) as good or evil and to expect only good works from the good and evil works from the evil. But one can do evil and then good and then lapse again into evil: The glory of God is shown in good works done by sinners. The illusion that there are people wholly just, to whom performance of God's works is wholly reserved, derives from pharisaical hypocrisy or resolute disregard of reality.

God's glory has been transmitted to sinners, who must live in constant tension between sin and good works, between evil and glory. The history of the church shows that there never was a pure mission accomplished by saints. The increase of Christ's glory in the world has been accompanied by lies, opportunism, injustices, religious divisions and hatreds, torture, and murder—by all the corruptions of Christianity and the Word that modern critics have forced us to recognize. But amid the errors and wrongs God's works appeared and revealed his glory.

The history of evangelization in the Americas is a perfect case in point. The Gospel of life and peace reached the Americas by way of conquest, enslavement of entire peoples, and destruction of their societies and their cultures. The conquered indigenes were killed outright or worked to death; their places in the mines and plantations were filled with enslaved Africans. The Gospel has been stained for all time by its historical association with the crimes of conquest. But even in that dreadful context Jesus' works were accomplished and manifested his glory to the faithful.

The mission must not wait for ideal conditions: If it awaited them, it would never begin. The mission does not need superhumans: If it did, it would never be carried out. We must not wait for a specifically "favorable" historical context, for there is no such thing; all historical moments, each in its own way, require and conduce to Christian mission.

Missionaries are called upon to act in adverse social and cultural contexts within a church whose institutions teem with ambiguity and equivocation. Associated with people whose conduct contradicts, always, the message they want to transmit, they are also painfully conscious of the contradictions between their own actions and their message.

But God's glory is not constrained by these conditions. Stronger than all corruptions, it manifests itself when it wills. The Father can reveal his glory even through unworthy intermediaries. All human intermediaries are by definition unworthy, but alongside their evil works shine the works of the Spirit. Of the men that evangelized the Americas, some were better and some worse, and most were an unpredictable mixture of good and evil. Reserve God's work to the perfectly just and which of us could do it? Even Peter denied Jesus three times and was nevertheless called to glorify God:

> "And further, I tell you this in very truth: when you were young you fastened your belt about you and walked where you chose; but when you are old you will stretch out your arms, and a stranger will bind you fast, and carry you where you have no wish to go." He said this to indicate the manner of death by which Peter was to glorify God (21:18–19).

For sinners are also capable of sublime works, and the publican can be as much or more a missionary than the Pharisee.

Missionaries, like Peter, succeed when

others take them where they had not thought or wished to go. Forces beyond themselves bring them to fulfill works they never dreamed of. And in like manner forces beyond themselves undo their most carefully conceived projects. When missionaries mistake their own will for God's glory, their works, however pious and altruistic they seem, are bound to fail. Only those works that really glorify the Father come to fruition in history, and in all of them we encounter the meaning of the cross. Most often, these are the works not valued or honored but discounted and despised among people; but it is precisely these works in which Christ is exalted and the Father glorified and the mission continued. "You did not choose me: I chose you. I appointed you to go on and bear fruit, fruit that shall last" (15:16).

5

"Grace and truth"

BORN FROM SPIRIT

Jesus was sent to manifest the Father's glory, which is that people have life: "that through this faith you may possess life by his name" (20:31). The purpose of mission is that the world have life. Life was the beginning of the world and will be its end; "all that came to be was alive with his life, and that life was the light of men" (1:4).

"Life" is one of the principal themes of the Fourth Gospel. Sometimes John calls it "eternal life," sometimes simply "life." It signifies, first, the final resurrection at the end of time:

> In very truth I tell you, a time is coming, indeed it is already here, when the dead shall hear the voice of the Son of God, and

all who hear shall come to life.... The
time is coming when all who are in the
grave shall hear his voice and come out:
those who have done right will rise to life
(5:25,29).

I am the bread of life. Your forefathers
ate the manna in the desert and they are
dead. I am speaking of the bread that
comes down from heaven, which a man
may eat and never die. I am that living
bread which has come down from heaven;
if anyone eats this bread he shall live
forever (6:48–51).

The raising of Lazarus emphasized this
meaning: "I am the resurrection and I am life.
If a man has faith in me, even though he die, he
shall come to life; and no one who is alive and
has faith shall ever die" (11:25).

The life that comes from Jesus, however, is
not limited to the future resurrection; it also
comprises "this" life, or life in the historical
world. The future life is none other than the
fulfillment of this present life truly lived.
Jesus spoke of the future life as the plenitude
of this life. "To live," in terms of mission, is not
just to be present in the world. It is to realize in
oneself the full potentiality for good that is
human nature: "I have come that men may
have life, and may have it in all its fullness"

(10:10). To live like that in this world is to be already embarked upon eternal life: "Anyone who gives heed to what I say and puts his trust in him who sent me has hold of eternal life, and does not come up for judgement, but has already passed from death to life" (5:24).

Passages in John referring to life are too numerous to catalogue. Almost all the attributes of Jesus' glory allude to life: He is the light of life, the bread of life, the way and the life, the shepherd and life. Life is the quintessence of the Gospel message, distinguishing it from all other religions. Other religions subordinate humanity to the service of their gods: The Jews, for example, conceived of themselves chiefly as executors of religious laws. Jesus proclaimed God's will to be not human obedience but human life, present and eternal. The Gospel message thus precludes religious alienation.

We must recognize that what is often called Christianity bears no resemblance to Christ's message. Too many "professing Christians" profess what Jesus utterly opposed—a new law, a new pharisaism. Why should this be? Because many professing Christians know of their religion only what was taught them as children and never attain to an adult understanding of Jesus' revelation. All their lives they profess a childish religion, doing obeisance to a god who commands and reprimands, who prohibits, monitors, and punishes—a god by whom they are dominated and from whom they are alienated, a god whom they fear.

But the Father's glory is the life of human-kind: That is the sum and substance of the Fourth Gospel.

The nature of this life is not self-evident; it requires definition. It is not a life withdrawn from this world into cultic observance and artificial purity. Such an unreal life is a constant temptation to contemplatives and, in its modern and secularized version, to revolutionaries who, impatient of the world's corruption and ambiguities, seek diverse radical purities that are by definition inhuman and therefore illusory. The historical life of which Jesus spoke is life within this world.

What most people have always called life, however, although all too real, negates God's will and human potential. Life in the world as Jesus would have it entails so drastic a transformation of our perception and our conduct as to warrant calling it (as Jesus did) a new life and attributing it to a new birth: "Unless a man has been born over again he cannot see the kingdom of God" (3:3). To be born again is to be invested by the Spirit: "Flesh can give birth only to flesh; it is Spirit that gives birth to spirit" (3:6).

"You ought not to be astonished, then,
when I tell you that you must be born over
again. The wind blows where it wills; you
hear the sound of it, but you do not know
where it comes from, or where it is going.
So with everyone who is born from spirit"
(3:7–8).

"The spirit alone gives life; the flesh is of
no avail; the words which I have spoken to
you are both spirit and life" (6:63).

"Streams of living water shall flow out
from within him." He was speaking of the
Spirit which believers in him would receive later (7:38–39).

In the new life that commences upon being
reborn in the Spirit one is a child of God: "not
born of any human stock, or by the fleshly
desire of a human father, but the offspring of
God himself" (1:13).

The Spirit that inspired Jesus' words inspires all who receive it, and so unites them to
Jesus. Rebirth in the Spirit enables one to perceive the Father's love and to love others; that
ability is simultaneously the result, the indi-
cation, and the meaning of rebirth: "I will ask
the Father, and he will give you another to be
your Advocate, who will be with you forever
—the Spirit of truth. The world cannot receive
him, because the world neither sees nor knows

him . . ." (14:16–17). The Spirit opens the
human spirit to perfect truth, the truth of
Jesus Christ (14:26; 15:26; 16:13).

The new life is not a message for children;
Jesus' message was and is proclaimed to adults
adapted to "the world," that is, to a self-
centered and self-serving existence. But Jesus
taught not existence but life, meaning relin-
quishment of all defense against others and
against the truth. Institutional Christianity
has betrayed him, making his teaching the
cornerstone of yet another ideology that es-
tranges people from God, truth, and one
another, but the teaching itself remains clear
in the Gospel.

Jesus proposed no specific task or test whose
accomplishment qualified people for rebirth or
marked them as reborn. He specified no cult,
no temples, no ceremonies, no prescribed actions. He called upon people to assume the responsibility of interpreting their times and
their conditions according to God's will and to
live according to their interpretations. How
much easier, how much more secure, to have a
prescribed and delimited task than to have
total responsibility for one's being here and
now! Our ideologies are fertile in providing us
with "causes"—country, family, class, science,
art—for which to sacrifice ourselves and by
which to persuade ourselves that we are truly
alive. But Jesus unmasked all our causes as

security blankets. No cause is justified in itself; therefore it cannot justify our existence.
It is our way of living that must justify our
causes.

FAITH IN HIM

Faith is the act that inaugurates rebirth
into a new life, and it is also the defining
characteristic of the new life. The "act of
faith," however, is not a discrete, delimited
action or avowal; it is a state of permanent
transformation, a new way of being that oper-
ates in all the diverse circumstances and
events of life.

Faith and life are linked by John throughout
the Gospel:

To those who have yielded him their allegiance, he gave the right to become children of God (1:12).

Those [signs] here written have been recorded in order that you may hold the
faith that Jesus is the Christ, the Son of
God, and that through this faith you may
possess life by his name (20:31).

This Son of Man must be lifted up as the
serpent was lifted up by Moses in the wilderness, so that everyone who has faith in
him may in him possess eternal life. God
loved the world so much that he gave his

only Son, that everyone who has faith in him may not die but have eternal life (3:14–16).

He who puts his faith in the Son has hold of eternal life (3:36).

These and many more texts relating faith to life reveal that this relationship is an essential aspect of mission.

Missionaries must never lose sight of the purpose of their mission, which is life. Their purpose is not universal observance of any law or cult; it is that people live to the fullest bent of their humanity, so that their lives testify to their creation in God's image. The awakening to life is faith, and the missionary's work is to open people's eyes to faith. It is not the missionary's work to furnish people with a program of action, yet that is the permanent temptation of all apostles. The essence of clericalism is "to help," "to orientate," "to mold," to make decisions for people—all "for their own good." This is the "temptation to do good"; in reality good comes about only if people assume responsibility for bringing it about themselves. The missionaries who try to act as parents or educators have lost sight of their mission, which is to reveal God's will, which is life.

If faith is the essential origin and characteristic of life, then we must understand it correctly. John enables us to understand: He depicts faith by narrating sympathetic responses to Jesus' works, just as he depicts mission by narrating selected examples of the works themselves.

The faith John depicts is of two kinds, and the distinction between them is of the greatest importance. The people who believed in Jesus because of the signs believed in him as a protector, as one who would point the way, tell them what to do, in a word, relieve them of their moral responsibilities and assume the burden of their lives. Such belief is a kind of first step to faith, a preliminary heedfulness, but no more. Such faith is not the stuff of which disciples are made, and Jesus said so plainly and repeatedly.

To Nathanael Jesus said: "Is this the ground of your faith, that I told you I saw you under the fig-tree? You shall see greater things than that" (1:50). Nathanael eventually attained true faith, but not all who believed in the signs could transcend that childish belief as he did: "While he was in Jerusalem for Passover many gave their allegiance to him when they saw the signs that he performed. But Jesus for his part would not trust himself to them" (2:23–24). Those people gave credence to Jesus' miracles, but they were not awakened by the miracles to comprehension of Jesus' reality or the reality of life. They saw wonders, but the purpose of the wonders escaped them.

Nicodemus arrived at the same imperfect faith: "Rabbi," he said, "we know that you are a teacher sent by God; no one could perform these signs of yours unless God were with him" (3:2), but the conversation that followed shows that Nicodemus did not understand Jesus' mission.

The Samaritan woman credited Jesus with the gift of prophecy (4:19), but her astonished outburst was not yet a confession of faith. The Galileans were moved to a similar enthusiasm by the multiplication of the loaves and fishes—"Surely this must be the prophet that was to come into the world" (6:14)—but Jesus, far from calling them to become disciples, hid from their naive and superficial ardor.

Much later,

as the Jewish Feast of Tabernacles was close at hand, his brothers said to him, "You should leave this district and go into Judaea, so that your disciples there may see the great things you are doing. Surely no one can hope to be in the public eye if he works in seclusion. If you really are doing such things as these, show yourself to the world" (7:2–4).

Their belief in the signs was obvious; their understanding of Jesus' mission—i.e., their faith—was nil.

Even the disciples, like Thomas after the Resurrection, reverted sometimes from faith to a childish questing after signs: "Because you have seen me you have found faith. Happy are they who never saw me and yet have found faith" (20:29). By contrast, Peter expressed true faith when he refused to leave Jesus: "Lord, to whom shall we go? Your words are words of eternal life" (6:68).

The man born blind stands as perhaps the most complete model of simple and authentic faith. " 'Have you faith in the Son of Man?' The man answered, 'Tell me who he is, sir, that I should put my faith in him.' 'You have seen him,' said Jesus; 'indeed it is he who is speaking to you.' 'Lord, I believe,' he said, and bowed before him" (9:35–36).

Martha too had faith in Jesus: "Lord, I do, . . . I now believe that you are the Messiah, the Son of God who was to come into the world" (11:27).

Acknowledging the signs, or miracles, is not faith. Faith is a response to the manifestation of Jesus' glory. But not all responses were genuine faith. Faith did not consist in making Jesus a king. Neither does it consist in making him a symbol of social order and tranquillity:

Jesus was not sent to be founder of "Christian civilization." That is not faith but faith's opposite. The Pharisees made Moses a symbol of social order and tranquillity. Moses, who was the precursor of Christ, they made into Christ's adversary.

Faith in Jesus is not dependency or facile emotionalism or philosophy. It is not a substitute for science or for conscience. People have attempted to define it in all these ways, but these are self-serving deformations rather than correct definitions. Faith is a recognition, a knowing that Jesus was sent by God. By emphatic diction and by repetition the Gospel stresses this theme of "knowing."

THEY KNOW ME

To know Jesus is to know the Father. But no one knows the Father simply through personal experience, through reflection, or through observation of external reality. The truth about the Father remains hidden from people's eyes because we naturally project our desires and fears, our anguish and jealousy, onto God: "No one has ever seen God; but God's only Son, he who is nearest to the Father's heart, he has made him known" (1:18).

"The world . . . did not recognize him" (1:10), but the disciples knew him—or rather those who knew him received the name of disciples.

Jesus called them not wise men (those who
know) but disciples (those who learn) because
"wise man" implies teacher and no one can be
a teacher of the science of Jesus Christ. All are
students; all are always beginners. Nevertheless, they did come to know. But it is important
to understand what kind of knowledge they
came to have. As the Samaritans said to the
woman who showed them Jesus: "It is no
longer because of what you said that we believe, for we have heard him ourselves; and we
know that this is in truth the Savior of the
world" (4:42). That is not a statement of dogma
but of faith: They recognized Jesus in their
spirit.

All enduring insights and convictions eventually become institutionalized. Use and repetition convert intuitions into formalisms.
Faith is placed in formulas. The congregation
of believers metamorphoses into a congregation of churchgoers, whose members define
and maintain their group identity and coher-
ence by devising a formula—an orthodoxy—in
which to believe. Faith is of little use to institutions, but orthodoxy is all-important: the
members' understanding is dispensable, but
their assent to the institution's orthodoxy
is imperative for the institution's survival.
Creed replaces faith, routine replaces ardor
—even in groups that originated in comprehension and fervent conviction. The expla-

nation of this seemingly inevitable and certainly common transformation is not far to seek: Most people crave security and find thinking painful; assenting to a group orthodoxy supplies security and relieves them of the need to think.

Christian history excellently illustrates that melancholy pattern, although schisms have fractured one orthodoxy into many. To the superficial observer orthodoxy appears to be faith in the highest degree, but in reality it is only attachment to an institution, an attachment that confers on its holders the psychological benefits of security and a feeling of communion. Because of these psychological rewards, orthodoxy can generate unreasoning conviction, total enthusiasm, unconditional attachment—in a word, fanaticism. But Jesus wanted from his disciples not fanaticism but faith, not unthinking adherence but true recognition. To know Jesus is to enter into spiritual communion with him, to receive communication of the Spirit from him. This knowing is an opening of the self to Jesus' revelation of himself.

Mission does not consist in propagating orthodoxy but in arousing faith, which is knowledge of Jesus Christ. That is its end, and ends, it is well known, influence the choice of means. To instill, maintain, or expand orthodoxy, the most useful means are child education, social pressure, and permeation of popular culture and communication. These means are exquisitely adapted to the propagation of any kind of orthodoxy but so inappropriate for the propagation of faith that their use is a sure symptom that orthodoxy and not faith is being served. Jesus himself shunned all of these means—social pressures, psychological reward, control of education, affiliation with popular culture. He simply proclaimed his message: "I am the good shepherd; I know my own sheep and my sheep know me—as the Father knows me and I know the Father . . ." (10:14–15).

When he knew his hour was near, Jesus summarized for the disciples what they knew: "You are my friends, if you do what I command you. I call you servants no longer; a servant does not know what his master is about. I have called you friends, because I have disclosed to you everything that I heard from my Father" (15:14–15). He repeated the same theme in his final prayer.

> I have made thy name known to the men whom thou didst give me out of the world. They were thine, thou gavest them to me, and they have obeyed thy command. Now they know that all thy gifts have come to

me from thee; for I have taught them all
that I learned from thee, and they have
received it: they know with certainty that
I came from thee; they have had faith to
believe that thou didst send me (17:6–8).

To know Jesus was to know the Father. This
is most fully stated in Jesus' famous dialogue
with Philip:

"I am the way; I am the truth and I am
life; no one comes to the Father except by
me. If you knew me you would know my
Father too. From now on you do know him;
you have seen him." Philip said to him,
"Lord, show us the Father and we ask no
more." Jesus answered, "Have I been all
this time with you, Philip, and you still do
not know me? Anyone who has seen me
has seen the Father. Then how can you
say, 'show us the Father'? Do you not believe that I am in the Father, and the
Father in me? I am not myself the source
of the words I speak to you: it is the Father
who dwells in me doing his own work"
(14:6–10).

To know Jesus is to recognize that he is the
Father's presence, the one sent from the
Father, in whom the Father placed all his
being. To know Jesus is to recognize God in

him: This requires a new vision of God and a new vision of Jesus' humanity.

It requires a new vision of God: God is not a fantasy imaged with the attributes of power and majesty and all in the created world that induces fear in people, but God is *in the form of Jesus*; God is as no one had ever imagined God before.

It requires a new vision of Jesus' humanity: We need not conjure up proper representations of the divine; God is present in the human Jesus.

Knowing Jesus is not at all like mastering a trade or an academic discipline: There are no concepts or doctrines or methodology or training involved. The disciples know Jesus and the Father directly and familiarly. They participated in Jesus, in the sense of feeling and understanding and reacting to people and events in ways similar to, though not identical with, Jesus' ways. Missionaries are not propagandists of a cause or a leader or a doctrine external to people. They are communicators of the knowledge of God, and their mission is to pass on to others their sense of familiarity with and participation in Jesus' ways of being.

To know is to know the truth, which is Jesus himself, and also to know that one can live in the truth. This is a far different definition of truth than is contained in most philosophies. What is it to live in the truth?

THE TRUTH WILL SET YOU FREE

The life of which Jesus spoke is knowing, and to know is to live in the truth. In the sense intended by the Fourth Gospel, all three categories are at once transcendent and immanent, because Jesus Christ's reality is part of but also surpasses the historical world. Jesus embodied in free and autonomous form the truth that civilization hid, suppressed, or confused. His being separated truth from lies, or reality from illusion, and revealed truth whole and uncontaminated.

The world acknowledged many partial truths but it did not know or want the whole truth, for the whole truth would have condemned it. Jesus called the Jews liars (8:55) although much that they said was true, because they made of these partial truths a structure or system that obscured the truth and was a lie. In Jesus was truth. To know Jesus was to enter into the world of truth, to be able to enter into total reality. Disciples can be wrong on any particular matter, but they cannot live in "the lie."

Jesus' truth is not a scientific or philosophic conclusion, nor is it a substitute for observation, experience, or reason. It is a category by which human activity may be rectified in accordance with their own deepest reality. Jesus embodied truth in a way that made possible for people henceforth to live in truth: He was "the true light" (1:9), "full of grace and truth" (1:14); "grace and truth came through Jesus Christ" (1:17).

Jesus was the truth. Truth is an element of all his attributes. He was "the true bread from heaven" (6:32), the "true vine" (15:1). To Pilate Jesus replied: "My task is to bear witness to the truth. For this was I born; for this I came into the world, and all who are not deaf to truth listen to my voice" (18:37).

> But the time approaches, indeed it is already here, when those who are real worshippers will worship the Father in spirit and in truth (4:23).

> The world cannot receive him [the Spirit of truth], because the world neither sees nor knows him . . . (14:17).

> When he comes who is the Spirit of truth, he will guide you into all the truth . . . (16:13).

> You shall know the truth, and the truth will set you free (8:32).

> Consecrate them by the truth; thy word is truth. As thou hast sent me into the world, I have sent them into the world, and for their sake I now consecrate myself, that they too may be consecrated by the truth (17:17–19).

Between mission and truth there is a twofold connection: The mission's object was to teach people the truth, and the mission was itself the truth. The truth is that the Father sent the Son into the world to establish the reality of all things. To participate in mission is to leave the lie and enter into the truth.

REMAIN IN ME

Discipleship is permanent. Recognizing the truth, knowing Jesus to be the Son, having faith—whatever one calls it, it is not a momentary event or state but a new and abiding condition of life. But abidance implies more than permanence or long duration. In this permanence, in this "remaining" in Jesus and the Father, disciples concretely experience faith, knowing, and truth. The Son's mission originated in the Father's love; the disciples know the Son and the Father by participating in that love—by "dwelling," or "remaining," or "abiding" in it. Jesus said so explicitly.

Dwell in me, as I in you. . . . He who dwells in me, as I dwell in him, bears much fruit; for apart from me you can do nothing. . . . As the Father has loved me so I have loved you. Dwell in my love. If you heed my commands, you will dwell in my love, as I have heeded my Father's com-

mands and dwell in his love. . . . This is my
commandment: love one another, as I
have loved you (15:4–12).

If you love me you will obey my commands; and I will ask the Father, and he
will give you another to be your Advocate,
who will be with you for ever. . . . You
know him, because he dwells with you and
is in you (14:15–17).

I give you a new commandment: love
one another; as I have loved you, so you
are to love one another. If there is this love
among you, then all will know that you are
my disciples (13:34–35).

The love that Jesus commanded is universal:
Neither its subjects nor its objects are re-
stricted to any particular kin or community.
All love of other people offers concrete experience and proof of discipleship. Thus in the
mission's beginning is its end. The mission
began in the Father's love, and as a "transmission" of that love, and love marks all its stages.
To know Jesus is to know the movement, or
transmission, of which he is the center, and the
only way to know it is to love.

That love can be but poorly defined in words;
only after experiencing the rebirth from
worldliness to discipleship can one perceive
and understand it. By way of definition one
can only say that love has nothing to do with

religious or cultural imperialism or with individual or collective self-regard. It is liberation from the prison of egocentrism into the current of love that Jesus opened into the world.

6

"For judgment"

THE WITNESSES

The Gospel of John is the first Christian text to synthesize the narration of Jesus' life and death, his glory, the disciples' rebirth, and the world's unbelief within the concept of "judgment."

In its most obvious and superficial aspect this judgment was a process of law in which Jesus was accused of having broken the Mosaic law, brought before a tribunal, and condemned. But the real judgment was given by the Father and was exactly the opposite: By the Resurrection, the condemned Jesus was vindicated and his accusers stood condemned, or rather, self-condemned. The content of God's judgment, however, was pardon: The

Son came not to punish but to save. That pardon makes possible the world's rebirth into discipleship.

It is this thesis that determines the structure of John's Gospel. Let us examine the idea of judgment as John presents it.

Jesus himself referred to his mission as a judgment: "It is for judgment that I have come into this world" (9:39). To emphasize the paradoxical nature of this judgment he added, alluding to Isaiah, "to give sight to the sightless and to make blind those who see."

Being accused (of claiming falsely to be God's Son), Jesus invoked a witness—John the Baptist: "Your messengers have been to John; you have his testimony to the truth. Not that I rely on human testimony, but I remind you of it for your own salvation" (5:33–34). John's testimony is in fact cited repeatedly in the Fourth Gospel, though Jesus appealed to it himself only once. Sometimes it was offered gratuitously (1:15,36), sometimes in answer to questioning by the Pharisees or his own followers (1:19–34; 3:25–30), and in the introduction the Evangelist introduces the Baptist simply as one sent to bear witness to Christ: "There appeared a man named John, sent from God; he came as a witness ..." (1:6–7).

In addition to John the Baptist, Jesus called the Scriptures to witness on his behalf: "You study the Scriptures diligently, supposing that in having them you have eternal life;

. . . their testimony points to me . . ." (5:39).

For his third witness, Jesus called his own teachings:

> I have always taught in synagogue and in the temple, where all Jews congregate; I have said nothing in secret. Why question me? Ask my hearers what I told them; they know what I said (18:20–21).
>
> We speak of what we know, and testify to what we have seen, and yet you all reject our testimony (3:11).
>
> He who comes from heaven bears witness to what he has seen and heard, yet no one accepts his witness (3:31–32).

But the Pharisees, citing the law that only two witnesses other than the accused could provide a valid defense, said to him: "You are witness in your own cause; your testimony is not valid." Jesus replied, "My testimony is valid, even though I do bear witness about myself; because I know where I come from, and where I am going. You do not know either where I come from or where I am going" (8:13–14).

Since two witnesses were required, Jesus sought to provide them. His works, he said, were the Father's testimony on his behalf:

> But I rely on a testimony higher than John's. There is enough to testify that the

Father has sent me, in the works my Father gave me to do and to finish—the very works I have in hand. This testimony to me was given by the Father who sent me . . . (5:36–37).

In your own law it is written that the testimony of two witnesses is valid. Here am I, a witness in my own cause, and my other witness is the Father who sent me (8:17–18).

My deeds done in my Father's name are my credentials (10:25).

THE ACCUSATION

Jesus was at last formally charged before a Roman tribunal, but the law he was accused of breaking was the Mosaic law: "We have a law; and by that law he ought to die, because he has claimed to be Son of God" (19:7). His crime was blasphemy, for which he had narrowly escaped stoning and arrest before (10:31, 33).

Blasphemy was the last and gravest charge, but there had been others; any net that would hold the quarry would do. After the cure of the paralytic: "It was works of this kind done on the Sabbath that stirred the Jews to persecute Jesus" (5:16). Jesus invoked God as precedent for good works done on the Sabbath, but "this made the Jews still more determined to kill him, because he was not only breaking the

Sabbath, but by calling God his own Father, he claimed equality with God" (5:18).

Jesus' growing following among the lower classes could not be made a crime in law; but it was a potent agent of angry fear among the Establishment: "Is there a single one of our rulers who has believed in him, or of the Pharisees? As for this rabble, which cares nothing for the law, a curse is on them" (7:48–49). The prospect of losing their religious-juridical authority over "this rabble" was bad enough; the prospect of popular unrest triggering Roman reprisals was far worse, and it was this fear that finally doomed Jesus: "This man is performing many signs. If we leave him alone like this the whole populace will believe in him. Then the Romans will come and sweep away our temple and our nation" (11:48). To avert the danger to themselves, the Pharisees hastened to accuse Jesus of political ambition and to protect their loyalty to Roman order and autocracy: "We have no king but Caesar" (19:15). "If you let this man go, you are no friend to Caesar; any man who claims to be a king is defying Caesar" (19:12).

Out of the divine word revealed in the past the Pharisees fashioned an instrument for their own security—the charge of blasphemy —and supplemented it with the imputation of treason against Rome.

Jesus' trial and condemnation are the

world's hostility to God embodied in one historical moment. But the hostility has always existed, and it stands revealed again and again —in the persecution of the prophets before Jesus and of the disciples after him. All such episodes express John's theme: "The world . . . did not recognize him" (1:10).

THE HOUR

The "hour" refers to Jesus' condemnation to death. In fear and anger the Pharisees plotted his death (11:53), had him apprehended (18:1–11), brought him first before the high priest and then before Pilate for sentencing (18:28–38; 19:1–16), and finally took him away to execution (19:16–18). In all these events the Pharisees appear as initiators and agents and Jesus as resigned and passive victim. But the earthly judgment by which Jesus died was also an instrument of God's quite opposite judgment. It is true that Jesus died, and by the Pharisees' will, but his death, by which the Pharisees intended to eliminate him from history, placed him in reality in the center of history. What was intended on earth as supreme humiliation God intended as—and transformed into—exaltation.

Jesus' final defeat was his victory, and for this victory God chose the "hour." "My hour

has not yet come" (2:4), said Jesus in Cana. "At
this they tried to seize him, but no one laid a
hand on him because his appointed hour had
not yet come" (7:30); "yet no one arrested him,
because his hour had not yet come" (8:20).
Jesus himself always spoke of his hour, even in
anguish, as a glorification:

> The hour has come for the Son of Man to
> be glorified (12:23).
> Now my soul is in turmoil, and what am
> I to say? Father save me from this hour.
> No, it was for this that I came to this hour.
> Father, glorify thy name (12:27–28).
> It was before the Passover festival.
> Jesus knew that his hour had come and
> he must leave this world and go to the
> Father. He had always loved his own who
> were in the world, and now he was to show
> the full extent of his love (13:1).

And at the end of the prayer at the Last
Supper he said: "Father, the hour has come.
Glorify thy Son, that the Son may glorify
thee" (17:1).

Though Jesus seems, at the end, to have
been a passive victim of his enemies, John is at
pains to point out that everything happened as
the Father willed. "Thus the text of Scripture
came true: 'They shared my garments among

them, and cast lots for my clothing' " (19:24); "after that, Jesus, aware that all had come to its appointed end, said in fulfillment of Scripture, 'I thirst' " (19:28). The soldiers did not break his legs: "This happened in fulfillment of the text of Scripture: 'No bone of his shall be broken' " (19:36). John concludes his account of the Crucifixion in the same vein: "And another text says, 'They shall look on him whom they pierced' " (19:37).

All was foreordained by God. When Pilate, troubled and apprehensive, urged his authority over Jesus' fate as a reason for Jesus to speak, Jesus tranquilly responded, "You would have no authority at all over me . . . if it had not been granted you from above" (19:11).

God's judgment was Jesus' vindication and triumph; the interval is brief between his death and his Resurrection:

In a little while the world will see me no longer, but you will see me; because I live, you too will live (14:19).

You heard me say, "I am going away, and coming back to you." If you love me you would have been glad to hear that I was going to the Father; for the Father is greater than I. I have told you now, beforehand, so that when it happens you may have faith. I shall not talk much longer with you, for the Prince of this

world approaches. He has no rights over
me; but the world must be shown that I
love the Father, and do exactly as he
commands (14:28–31).

"A little while, and you see me no more;
again a little while, and you will see me" (16:16;
cf. 16:5–7,17–24). As a seed must lie in the
ground for the grain to grow, as a woman must
labor in pain for a child to be born, so, Jesus
told his disciples, he must depart to return in
"a little while" in eternal triumph:

> A grain of wheat remains a solitary
> grain unless it falls into the ground and
> dies; but if it dies, it bears a rich harvest.
> The man who loves himself is lost, but he
> who hates himself in this world will be
> kept safe for eternal life (12:24–25).
> In very truth I tell you, you will weep
> and mourn, but the world will be glad. But
> though you will be plunged in grief, your
> grief will be turned to joy. A woman in
> labour is in pain because her time has
> come; but when the child is born she
> forgets the anguish in her joy that a man
> has been born into the world. So it is with
> you: for the moment you are sad at heart;
> but I shall see you again, and then you will
> be joyful, and no one shall rob you of your
> joy (16:20–22).

Jesus' hour was the hour of victory: "The victory is mine; I have conquered the world" (16:33). It was the hour of exaltation:

This Son of Man must be lifted up as the serpent was lifted up by Moses in the wilderness, so that everyone who has faith in him may in him possess eternal life (3:14–15).

When you have lifted up the Son of Man you will know that I am what I am. I do nothing on my own authority (8:28).

I shall draw all men to myself, when I am lifted up from the earth (12:32).

Death and Resurrection compose one reality, and that reality John calls victory, or glory. Resurrection was a raising up from death and to glory, and the cross was the way to the Resurrection: "Father glorify thy name" (12:28; cf. 13:31, 17:1–5).

The "way of the cross" was in reality the way to the Father:

There are many dwelling-places in my Father's house; if it were not so I should have told you; for I am going there on purpose to prepare a place for you. And if I go and prepare a place for you, I shall come again and receive you to myself (14:2–3).

I am going to the Father (14:12).

If you loved me you would have been glad to hear that I was going to the Father (14:28).

I came from the Father and have come into the world. Now I am leaving the world again and going to the Father (16:28).

The judgment was concluded, its purpose accomplished.

THE JUDGMENT OF THE WORLD

God's judgment gave victory to Jesus, but what of the world? Does Jesus' victory mean the condemnation of the world?

Jesus' victory constituted the condemnation, not of the world, but of the "Prince of this world." His reign was over.

The Prince of this world approaches. He has no rights over me (14:30).

Now is the hour of judgement for this world; now shall the Prince of this world be driven out (12:31).

The Prince of this world stands condemned (16:11).

As to the world, Jesus did come not to judge it but to save it. God's justice is not a code of law; it is pardon and salvation. Only those who

reject his salvation judge and condemn themselves: those who reject the proffered light
must by definition remain in darkness: "It was
not to judge the world that God sent his Son
into the world, but that through him the world
might be saved. The man who puts his faith in
him does not come under judgement; but the
unbeliever has already been judged in that he
has not given his allegiance to God's only Son"
(3:17–18). Those who reject the unique font of
salvation that is the Son of God are thereby
condemned to be part of this world, cut off from
the light: "Here lies the test: the light has
come into the world, but men preferred darkness to light because their deeds were evil. Bad
men all hate the light and avoid it, for fear
their practices should be shown up. The honest
man comes to the light so that it may be clearly
seen that God is in all he does" (3:19–21).

But if anyone hears my words and pays
no regard to them, I am not his judge; I
have not come to judge the world, but to
save the world. There is a judge for the
man who rejects me and does not accept
my words; the word that I spoke will be his
judge on the last day (12:47–48).

Those who hear the word and do not accept
it are thereby judged.

The Father does not judge anyone, but has given full jurisdiction to the Son. ... Anyone who gives heed to what I say and puts his trust in him who sent me has hold of eternal life, and does not come up for judgement, but has already passed from death to life. ... The time is coming when all who are in the grave shall hear his voice and come out: those who have done right will rise to life; those who have done wrong will rise to hear their doom. I cannot act by myself; I judge as I am bidden, and my sentence is just, because my aim is not my own will, but the will of him who sent me (5:22–30).

The Pharisees, because they rejected the light, were self-condemned, and Jesus told them so: "You will die in your sin" (8:21); "if you do not believe that I am that what I am, you will die in your sins" (8:25). Their rejection of the light, which is life, made them willing to lie and to kill: "Your father is the devil and you choose to carry out your father's desires. He was a murderer from the beginning, and is not rooted in the truth; there is no truth in him. When he tells a lie he is speaking his own language, for he is a liar and the father of lies" (8:44). Precisely by bringing about Jesus' death, the Pharisees revealed their mendacity and murderousness; his death was their judgment.

For those who believed in his mission Jesus' death was pardon, salvation, eternal light and life, abiding with the Son and the Father: "I have not come to judge the world, but to save the world" (12:47). We have likened Jesus' life in the world to a judgment, but it more closely resembles the transformation of judgment into salvation. Jesus' life and death exemplify submission not to law but to love. His mission was not to threaten death but to offer life.

THE JUDGMENT OF THE DISCIPLES

The judgment does not end with Jesus' death and Resurrection, because Jesus' earthly mission has been carried on by his disciples. The judgment is continuously being re-enacted in the lives and works of the disciples.

Like Jesus, the disciples were not of the world but sent to the world:

> They are strangers in the world (17:14).
> I pray thee, not to take them out of the world, but to keep them from the evil one. They are strangers in the world, as I am (17:15–16).
> As thou hast sent me into the world, I have sent them into the world (17:18).

After his Resurrection Jesus told his disciples explicitly that he was entrusting his earthly mission to them: "As the Father sent me, so I send you" (20:21).

He told them, too, that the world would receive them as it had received him:

> They will ban you from the synagogue; indeed the time is coming when anyone who kills you will suppose that he is performing a religious duty. They will do these things because they do not know either the Father or me (16:2–3).
>
> If the world hated you, it hated me first, as you know well. If you belonged to the world, the world would love its own, but because you do not belong to the world, because I have chosen you out of the world, for that reason the world hates you.... As they persecuted me they will persecute you, they will follow your teaching as little as they have followed mine (15:18–20).

Mission is bound to arouse opposition, even persecution, because it uncovers the lies, the hate, and the murderousness that enslave the world. To uncover the world's sins is, in fact, essential to mission.

Herein lies the eternal challenge to the mission. Persecution does not, on the surface of things, seem like success, and the world offers tempting rewards for silent acquiescence in evil. There is no lack of pretexts and excuses for such silence. Of these, concern for the future of the church is the most insidious and takes two principal forms. One is so to institutionalize, ritualize, and formalize God's word that, though recited daily, it loses all meaning, all resonance in the world. The other is to overlook—discreetly—the evils done by the powerful, so as to avoid persecution or even destruction at their hands. Presumably the mission is thereby preserved for the future; actually it is only nullified in the present.

Obviously, the church has never officially abandoned God's Word. It celebrates it in its worship, proclaims it in its preaching, teaches it in its schools. But the Word can be celebrated in a way that is equivalent to silence. Proclaimed without reference or application to concrete historic realities, the Word engages no one because it denounces no real evil. The disciples were not sent to celebrate a cult but to make the world aware of its darkness by contrast with the light. If the world remains complacent, if its leaders feel no censure, is this not a sign that mission has been abandoned?

The disciples were called to give witness: "You also are my witnesses" (15:27). Their witness will be works: "In truth, in very truth I tell you, he who has faith in me will do what I am doing; and he will do greater things still . . ." (14:12). But their witness will also be the Word. For the Spirit will be in them and will inspire in them Jesus' message: "But when your Advocate has come, whom I will send you from the Father—the Spirit of truth that issues from the Father—he will bear witness to me" (15:26).

The disciples' words make present the testimony of Jesus in all generations, and of necessity they have the same effect. Far from lamenting the opposition between the church and the world, we must learn to recognize it as a sign of the church's fidelity to its mission. When the church is in harmony with the powers that be, it is betraying its mission, which is to present Jesus' message.

Within the mission as a whole, each one of us has a part to play. The form of our witness is determined by the circumstances we encounter. We cannot simply repeat Jesus' works by rote; we must communicate the Father's love for humankind in a way that is perceivable and comprehensible within our own historical context. If we can do that, we do not solve humanity's problems; we awaken people's consciences so that they can assume responsibility for their own lives.

Naturally we cannot separate the works of the disciples from other human endeavors to solve problems. The disciples, too, are members of human society, and their works are part of the total human effort. Nevertheless their efforts carry a certain Christian inspiration that tends to open up new paths to humanity.

Here our meditation on the Gospel of John comes to an end. Or rather our meditation on the written text ends here, but our meditation on the Gospel as lived by us begins. Where the written word ends the Spirit begins. The book of the Spirit was not written, but lived. The lives of generation upon generation of Christians are the living book of the Spirit, who inspires every generation with the appropriate witness. The Spirit cannot be confined to a book; it blows where it wills.

In the conflicts of today the Spirit is present, witnessing to the Son of God through the witness of the disciples. Examples are all around us of the words of the Spirit. But the world too is present, opposing the truth, the world with its oppression and lies, the world and its advocates, who, as in Israel of old, are often our leaders. Can we not ask today: "Is there a single one of our rulers who has believed in him?" (7:48). The difference is that today certain leaders have even learned to manipulate Jesus Christ himself, making him appear to say the opposite of what he truly says.

Nevertheless the word of God is present. Those who seek the light will discover it; they will discover the way of life: "The light shines on in the dark, and the darkness has never mastered it" (1:5).

Other Orbis Titles

GOD, WHERE ARE YOU?

by Carlos Mesters

Meditations and reflections on significant figures and events in the Bible. "We shall," says Mesters, "try to restore to the word of God the function that it ought to have: to serve as a light on the pathway of life, as a help to our own understanding of present-day reality in all its complexity."

ISBN 0-88344-162-4 CIP   *Cloth $6.95*

THE EXPERIENCE OF GOD

by Charles Magsam

"His range is comprehensive; his orientation is personal, biblical, communitarian; his tone is positive and encouraging: all in all, a one-volume course on how to be free wholesomely for God, for oneself and for others." *Prairie Messenger*

ISBN 0-88344-123-3   *Cloth $7.95*
ISBN 0-88344-124-1   *Paper $4.95*

JESUS OF NAZARETH

Meditations on His Humanity

by Jose Comblin

"St. Teresa of Avila warned her nuns to beware of any kind of prayer that would seek to eliminate all reference to the human aspect of Christ. I think Jose Comblin would agree that her warning also describes the theme of his extremely valuable book that can be read and re-read many times with great benefit." *Priests USA*

ISBN 0-88344-231-0   *Cloth $5.95*

PRAYER AT THE HEART OF LIFE

by Brother Pierre-Yves Emery

"Emery's approach is both realistic and down-to-earth and profound and moving. This book can be recommended to anyone interested in a practical analysis of prayer, particularly the specific relationship between prayer and life itself." *Review for Religious*

ISBN 0-88344-393-7   *Cloth $4.95*

PILGRIMAGE TO NOW/HERE

by Frederick Franck

"Every now and then a true gem of a book appears that fails to get caught up in the tide of promotion, reviews, and sales, and, despite its considerable merits, seems to disappear. Such a book is Dr. Frederick Franck's *Pilgrimage to Now/Here*. His *Zen of Seeing* has been a steady seller, and *The Book of Angelus Silesius* is moving well. What happened to *Pilgrimage*, which in many ways is a more important book? Since Orbis is known as a religious publishing house, many distributors and booksellers are reluctant to stock it. Yet this is a religious book in the most significant sense of that word—in what Frederick Franck would call the search for meaning—for it is an account of a modern pilgrimage by jet, bus, train, and on foot to visit holy places and meet Buddhist leaders and Zen masters in India, Ceylon, Hong Kong and Japan."

East West Journal

ISBN 0-88344-387-2   *Illustrated Paper $3.95*

BIBLICAL REVELATION
AND AFRICAN BELIEFS

edited by Kwesi Dickson and Paul Ellingworth

"Essays by scholars who are themselves both African and Christian and who share a concern that Christian theology and African thought be related to each other in a responsible and creative way. There is no comparable book; this one should be in any library attempting serious coverage of either African thought or Christian theology." *Choice*

ISBN 0 88344 033-4   *Cloth $5.95*

ISBN 0-88344-034-2   *Paper $3.45*

IN SEARCH OF THE BEYOND

by Carlo Carretto

"The book describes an 'aloneness' that draws hearts closer together, a 'withdrawal' that enriches family and community ties, a love of God that deepens human love." *America*

ISBN 0-88344-208-6   *Cloth $5.95*

LETTERS FROM THE DESERT

by Carlo Carretto

"It has been translated into Spanish, French, German, Portuguese, Arabic, Japanese, Czech, and now, gracefully enough (from Italian) into English. I hope it goes into twenty-four more editions. It breathes with life, with fresh insights, with wisdom, with love." *The Thomist*

ISBN 0-88344-279-5   *Cloth $4.95*

THE GOD WHO COMES

by Carlo Carretto

"This is a meaty book which supplies on every page matter for reflection and a spur to the laggard or wayward spirit. It offers true Christian perspective." *Our Sunday Visitor*

ISBN 0-88344-164-0   *Cloth $4.95*

FREEDOM TO BE FREE

By Arturo Paoli

"Full of eye-opening reflections on how Jesus liberated man through poverty, the Cross, the Eucharist and prayer." *America*

ISBN 0-88344-143-8   *Paper $4.95*

SILENT PILGRIMAGE TO GOD

The Spirituality of Charles de Foucauld

by a Little Brother of Jesus
preface by Rene Voillaume

"Sets out the main lines of Charles de Foucauld's spirituality and offers selections from his writings." *America*

ISBN 0-88344-459-3   *Cloth $4.95*

AFRICAN TRADITIONAL RELIGION: A DEFINITION

by E. Bolaji Idowu

"This important book is the first to place the study of African religion in the larger context of religious studies. . . . It includes an index and notes. There is no comparable work; this one should be in any collection on African religion." *Choice*

ISBN 0-88344-005-9   *Cloth $6.95*

THE PATRIOT'S BIBLE

edited by John Eagleson and Philip Scharper

"Following the terms of the Declaration of Independence and the U.S. Constitution, this faithful paperback relates quotes from the Bible and from past and present Americans 'to advance the kingdom and further our unfinished revolution.' " *A.D.*

ISBN 0-88344-377-5   *Paper $3.95*

THE RADICAL BIBLE

adapted by John Eagleson and Philip Scharper

"I know no book of meditations I could recommend with more confidence to learned and unlearned alike." *St. Anthony Messenger*

ISBN 0-88344-425-9   *Cloth $3.95*
ISBN 0-88344-426-7   *Pocketsize, paper $1.95*

UGANDA: THE ASIAN EXILES

by Thomas and Margaret B. Melady

"Takes its inspiration from the announcement in August 1972 by General Idi Amin Dada, President of Uganda, that he was told in a dream to order the expulsion of all Asians from Uganda. Tom and Margaret Melady were there and were witness to the tragic events. The book surveys the gruesome events following the expulsion order and the irrational pattern of Amin's record as well as providing a factual background of the Asian presence in Africa. The historical, economic and social complexity of the African-Asian-European situation in Uganda is made clear. Stories of personal devotion and heroism put flesh on the facts." *Religious Media Today*

ISBN 0-88344-506-9 CIP   *Cloth $6.95*